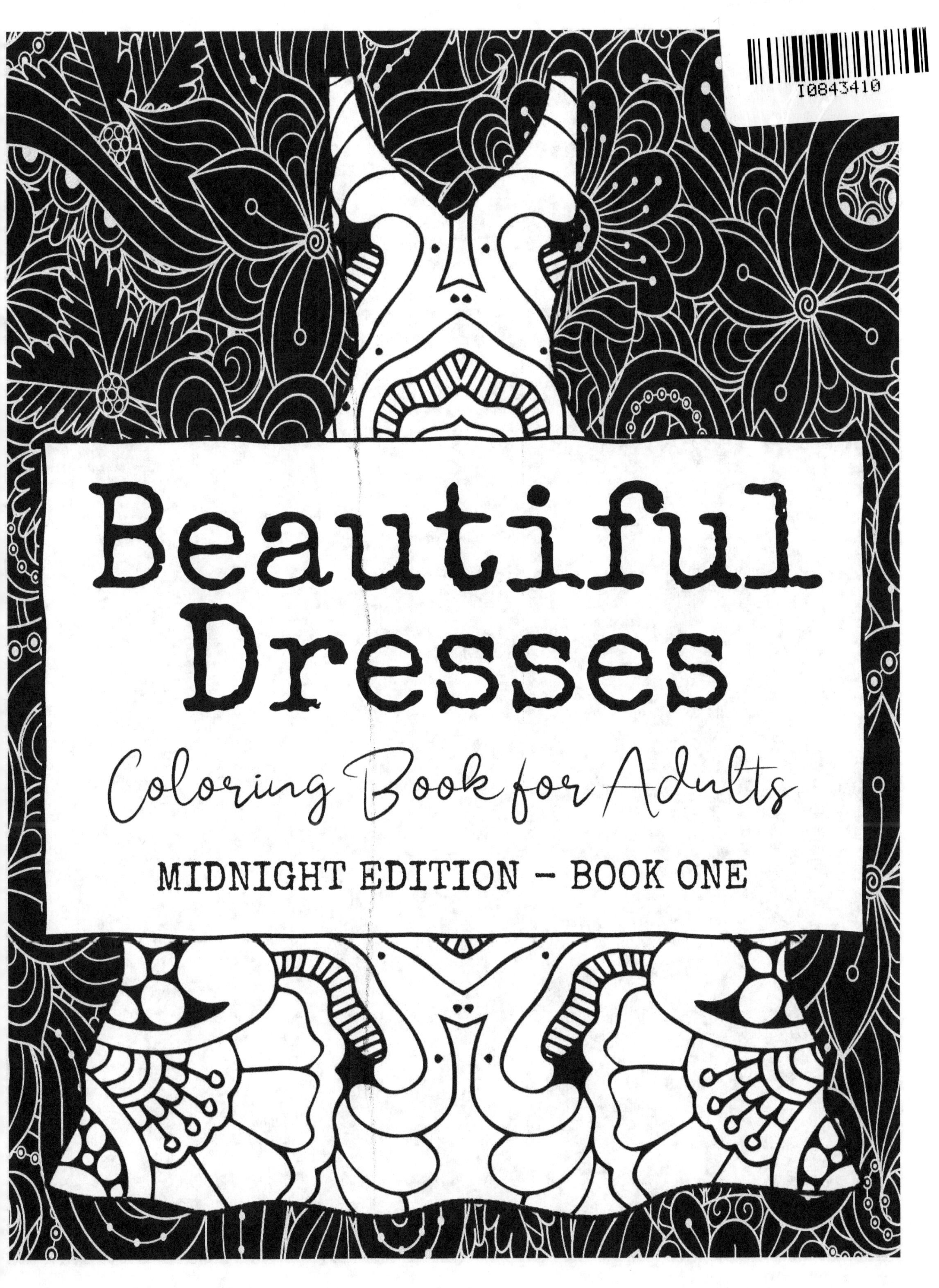
Beautiful
Dresses
Coloring Book for Adults
MIDNIGHT EDITION – BOOK ONE

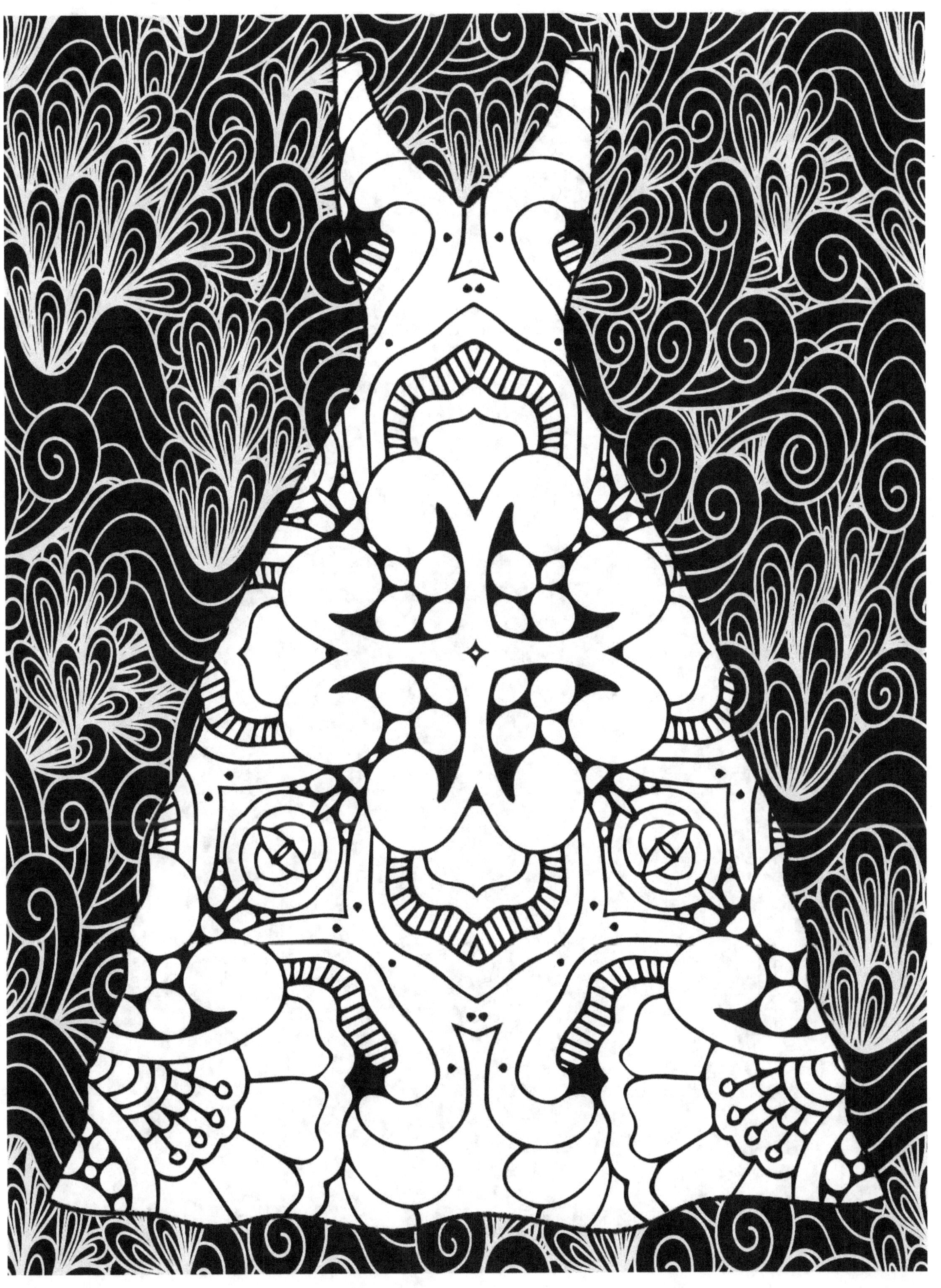

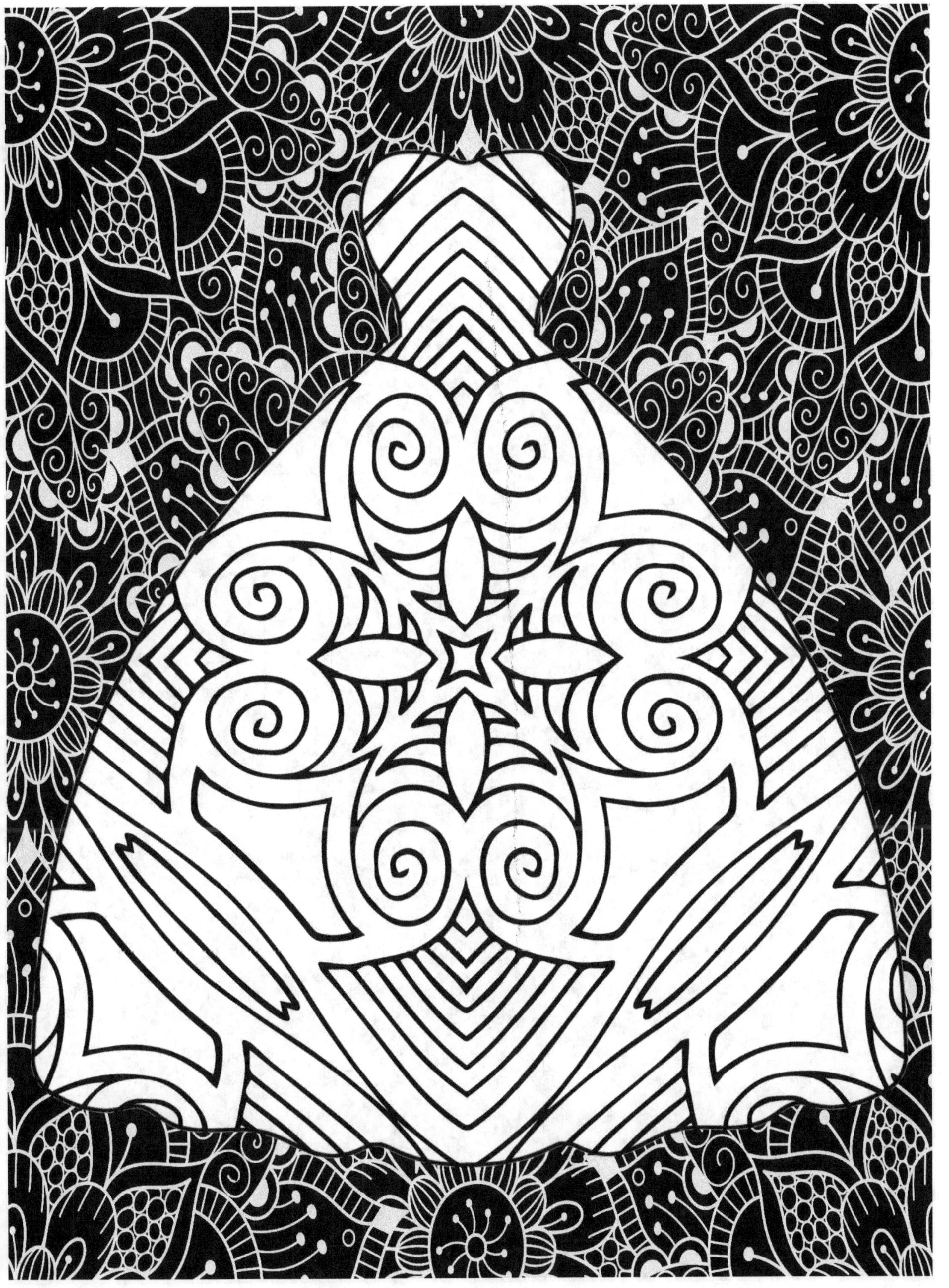

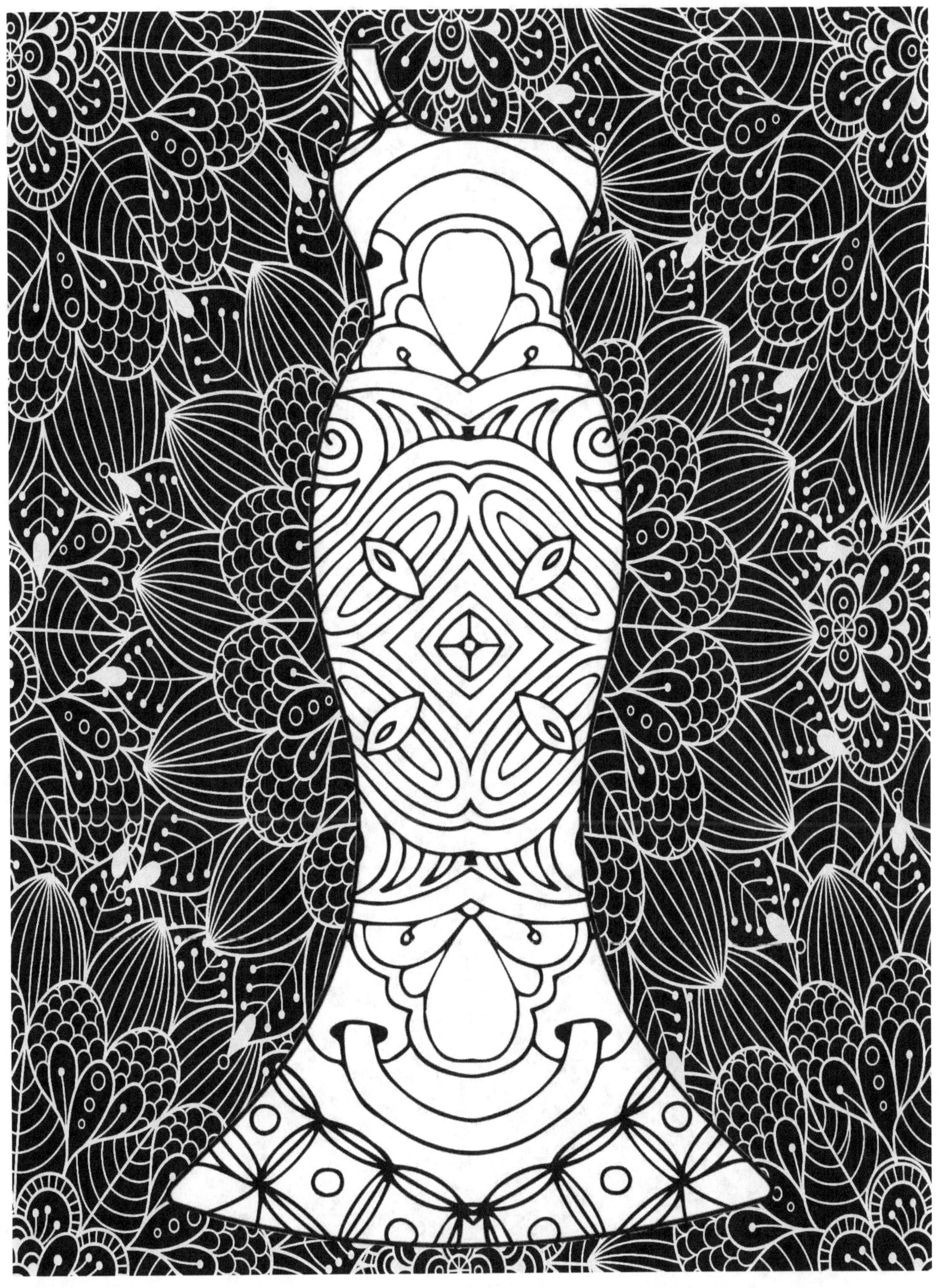

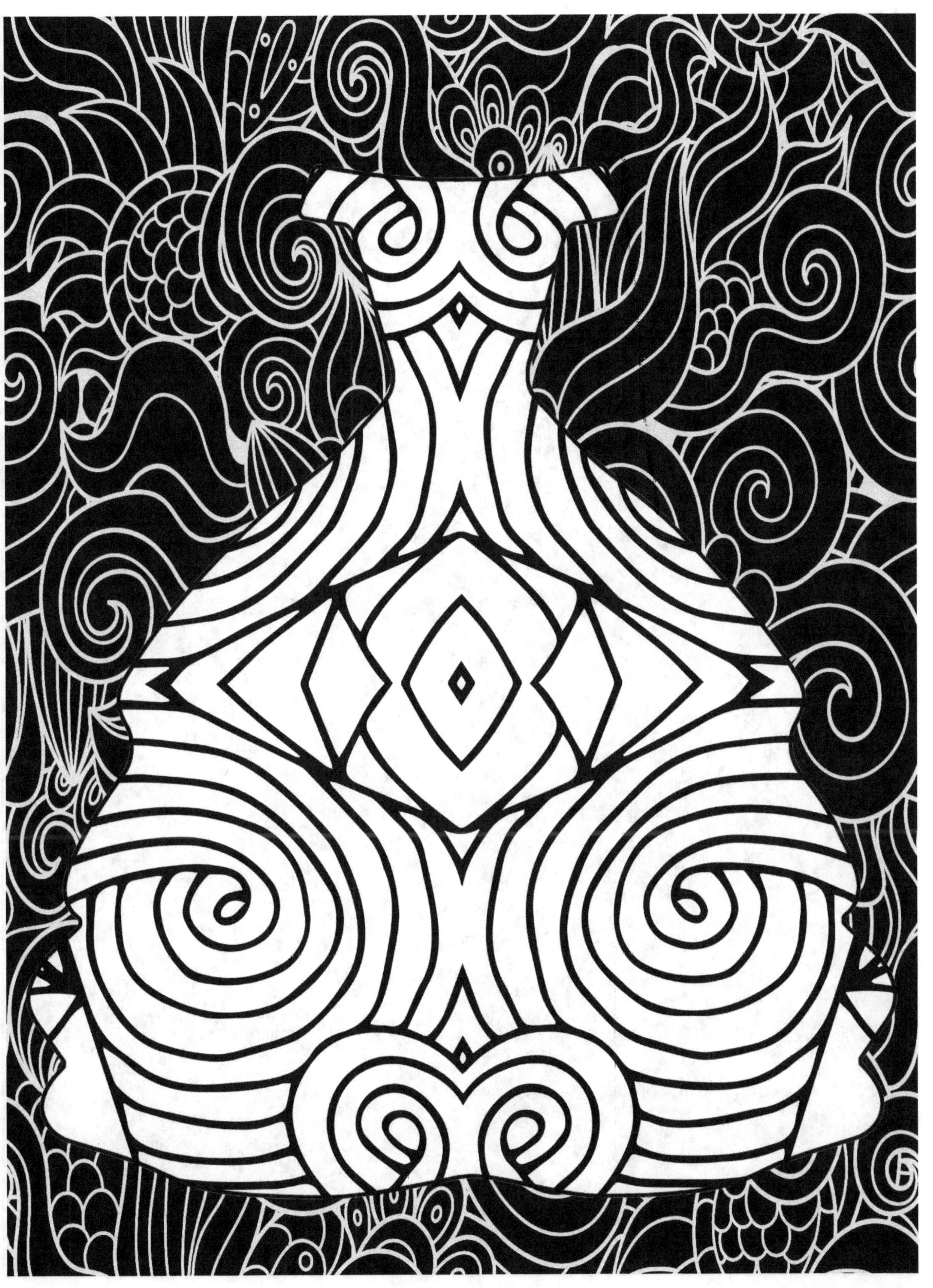

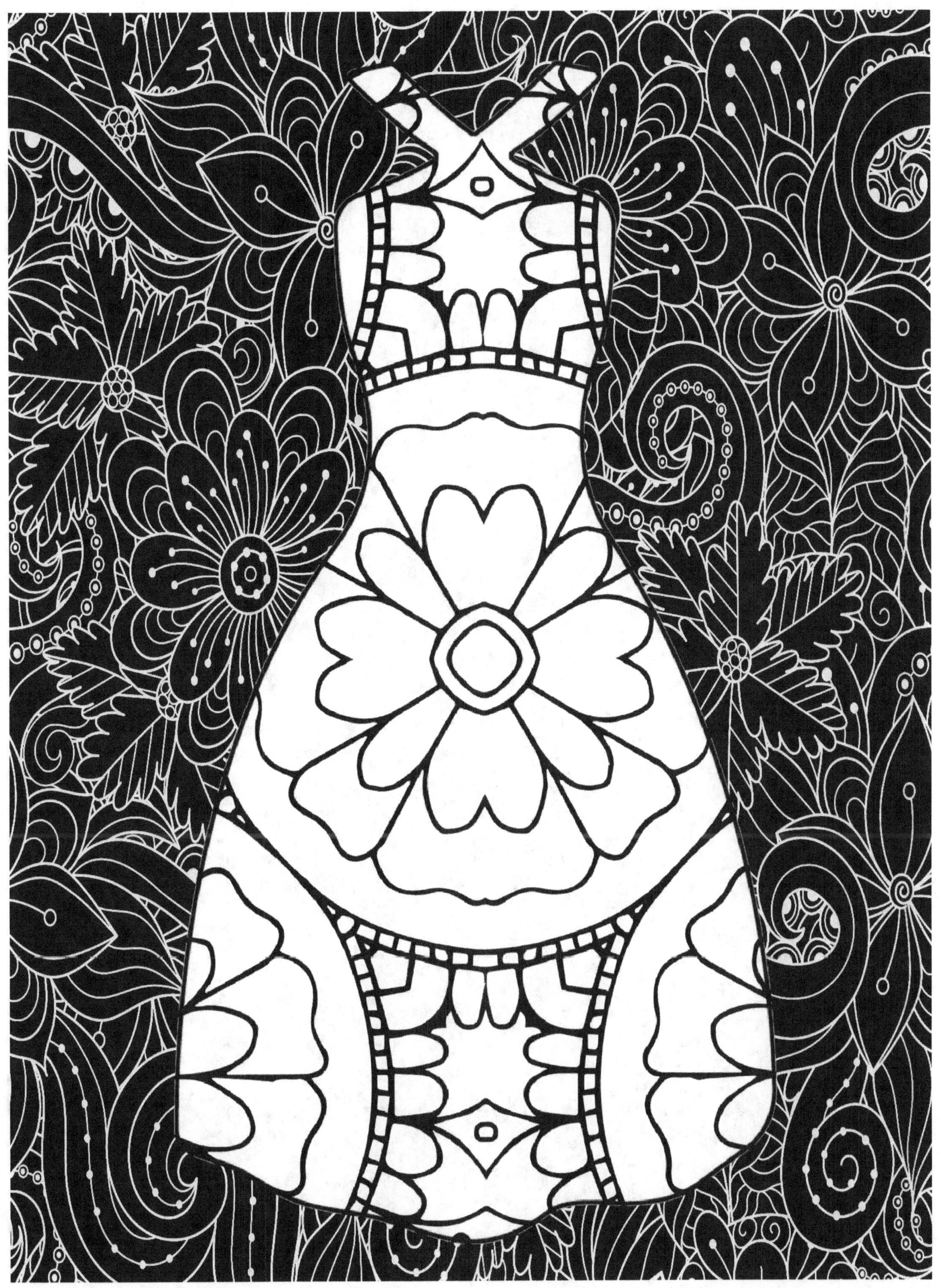

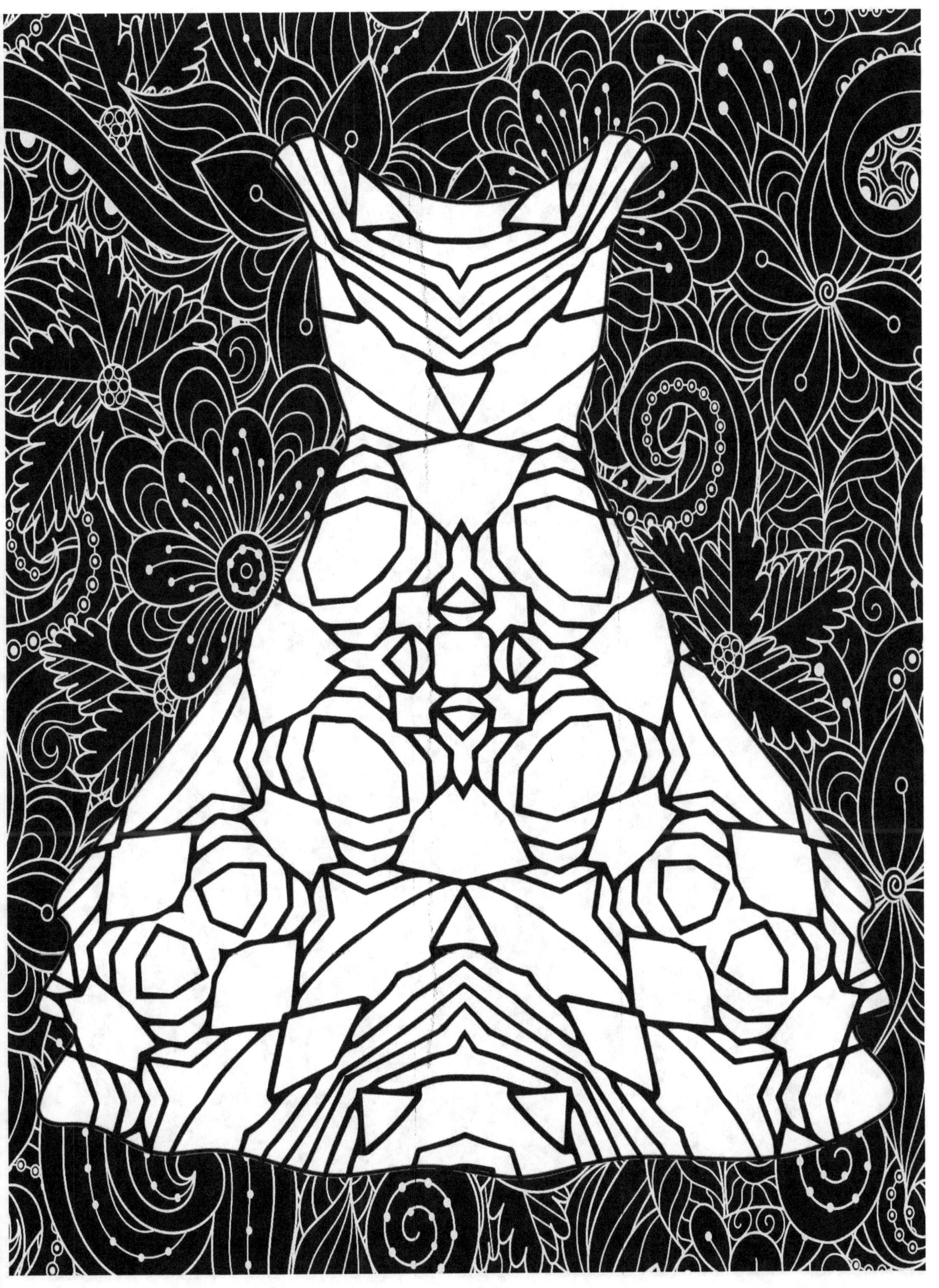

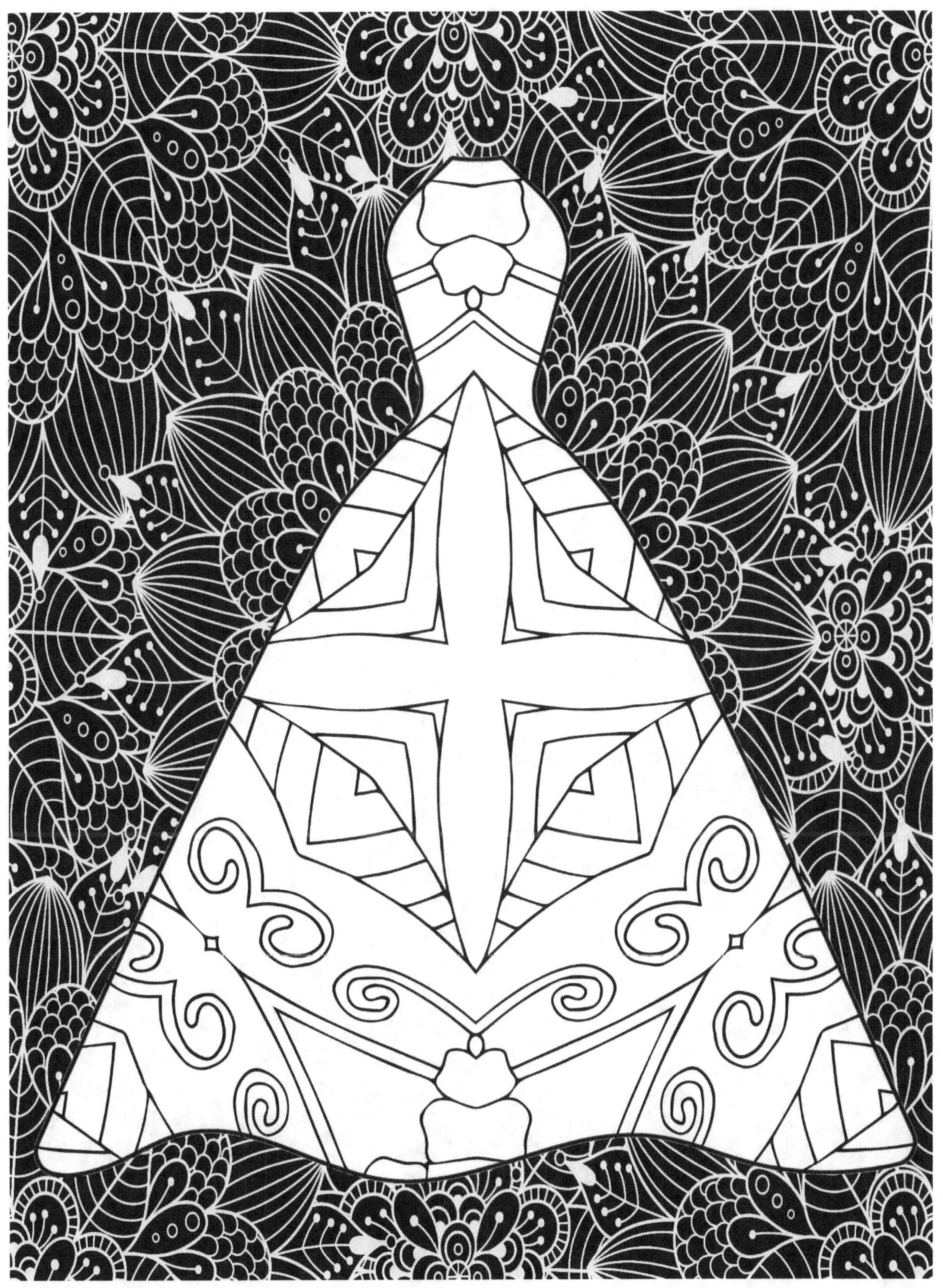

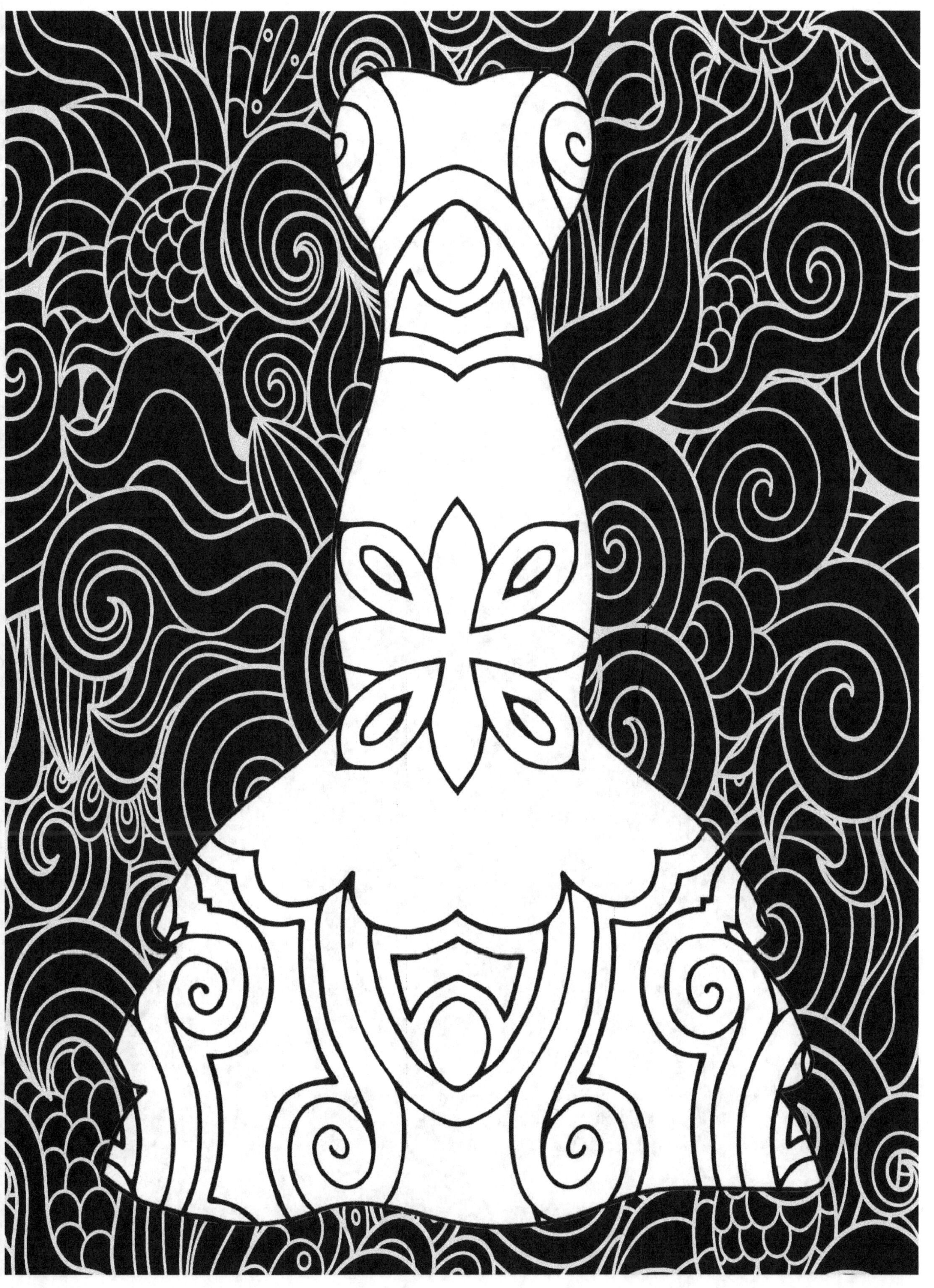

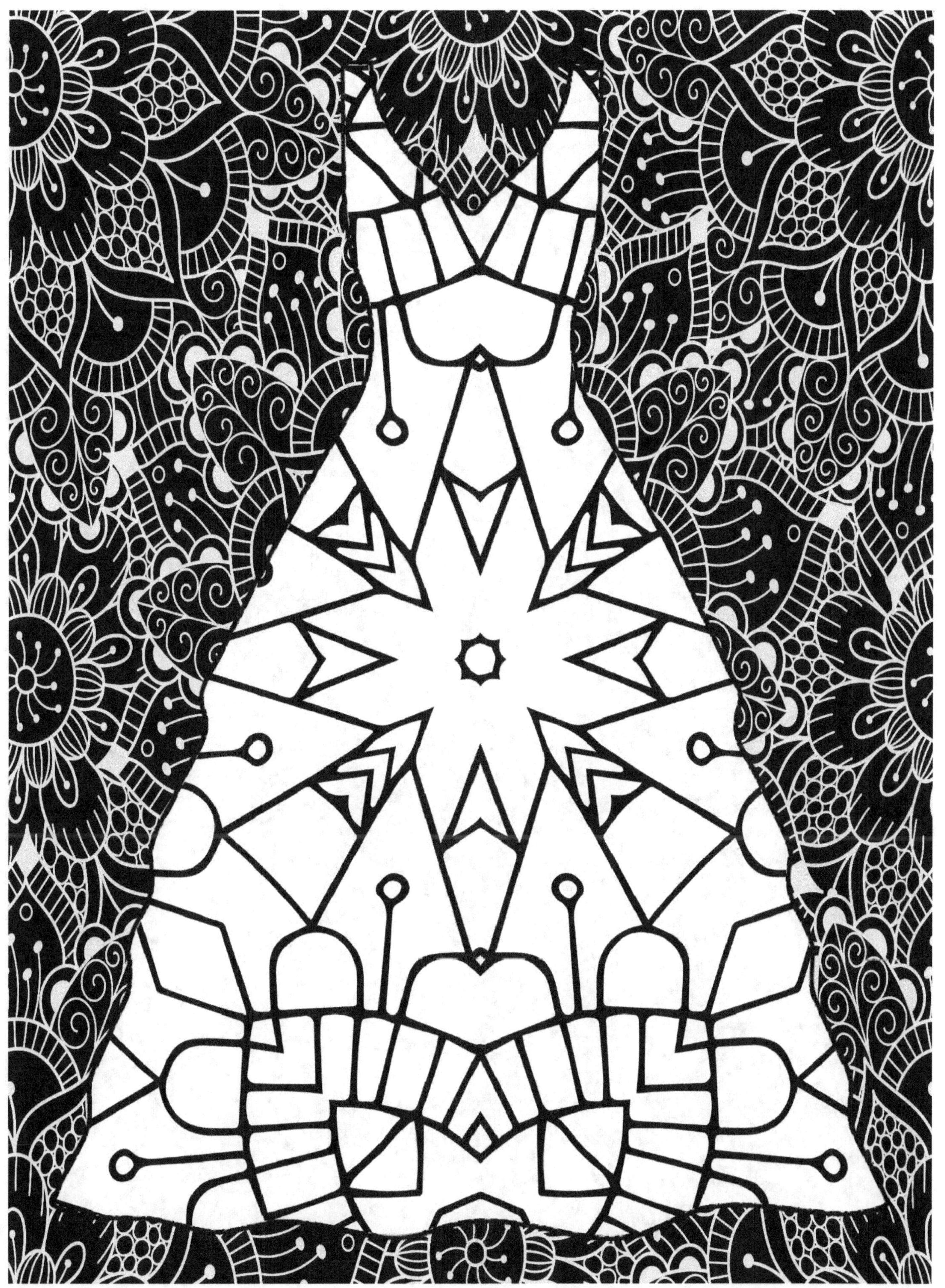

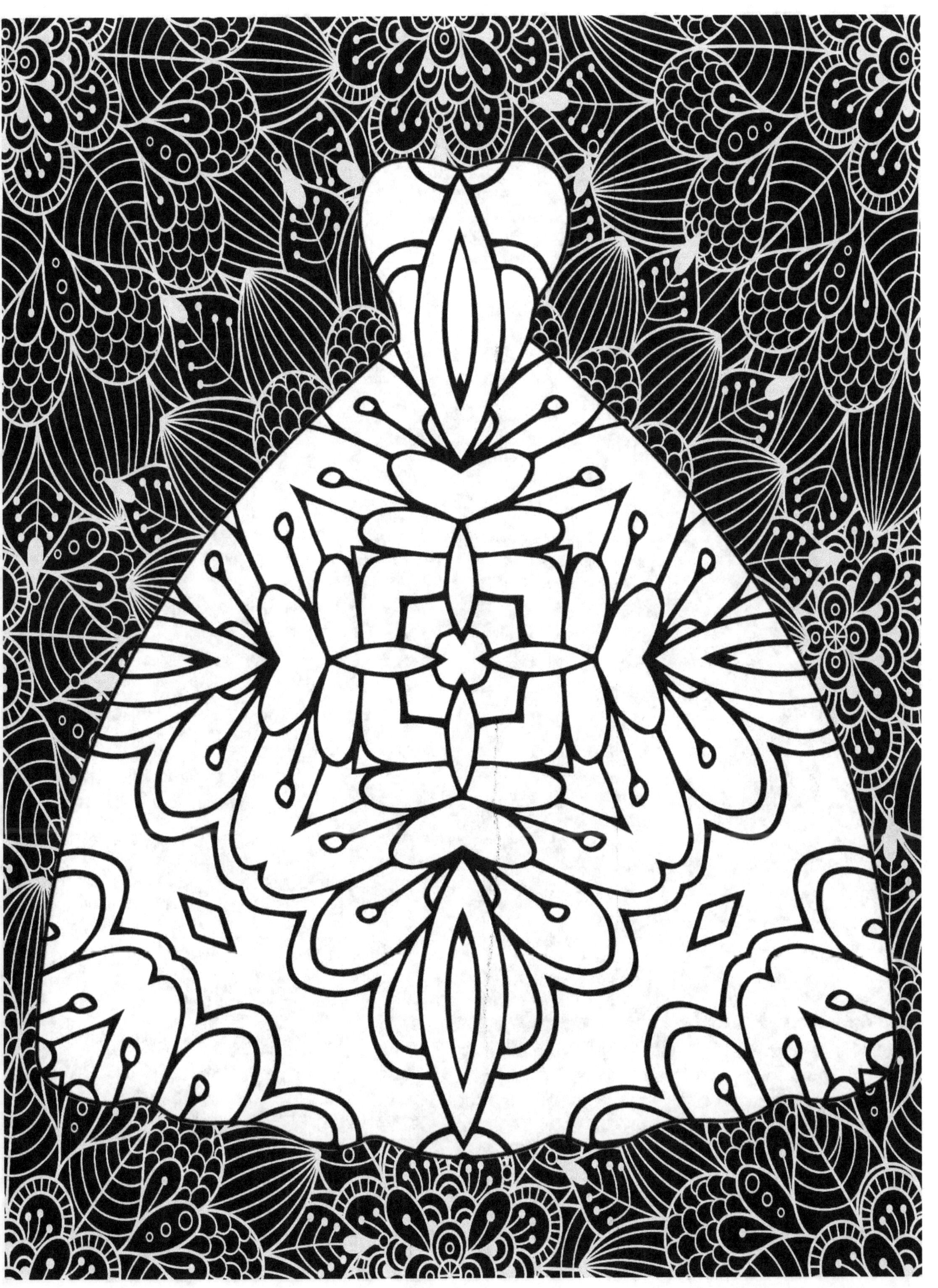

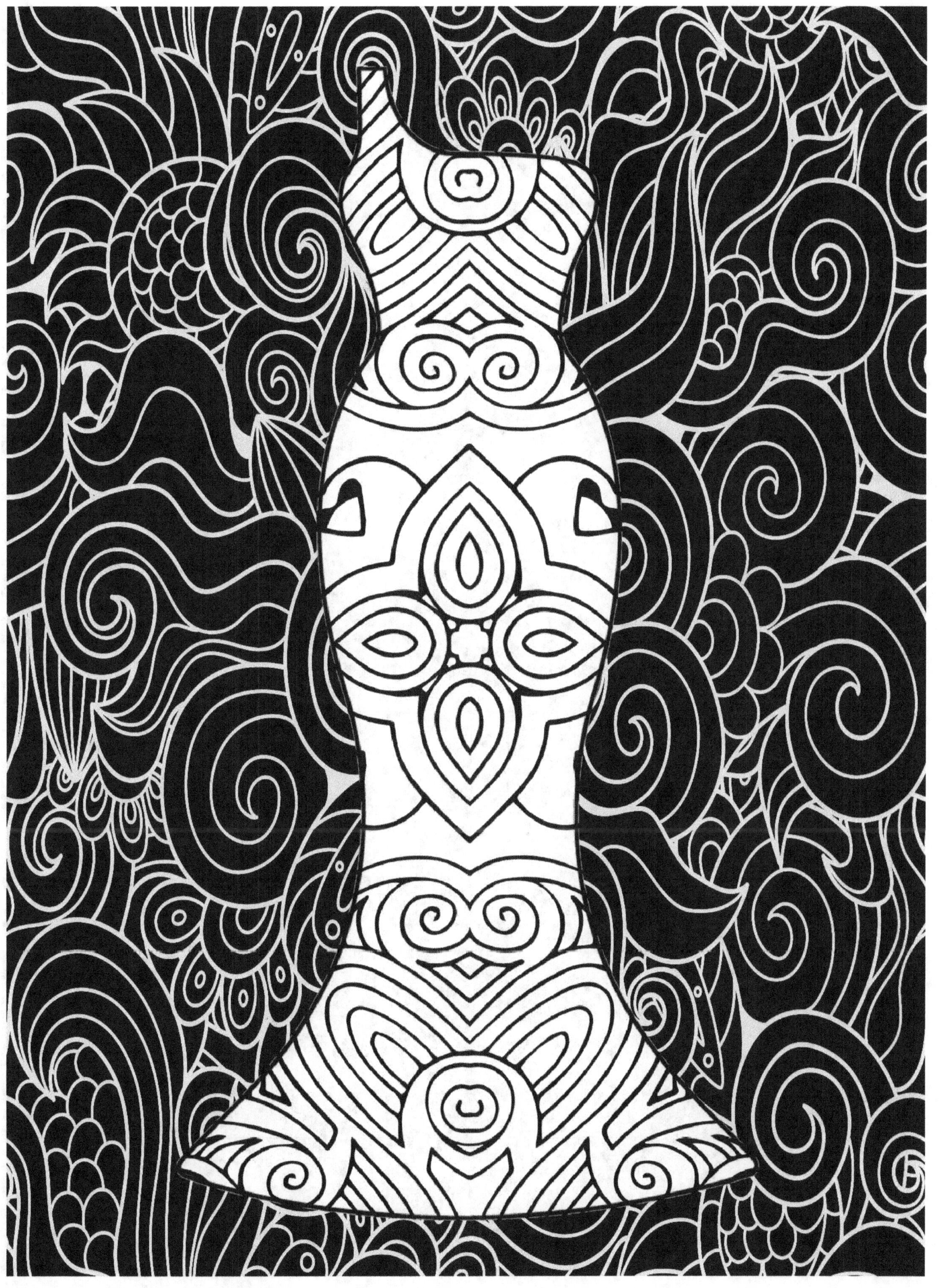

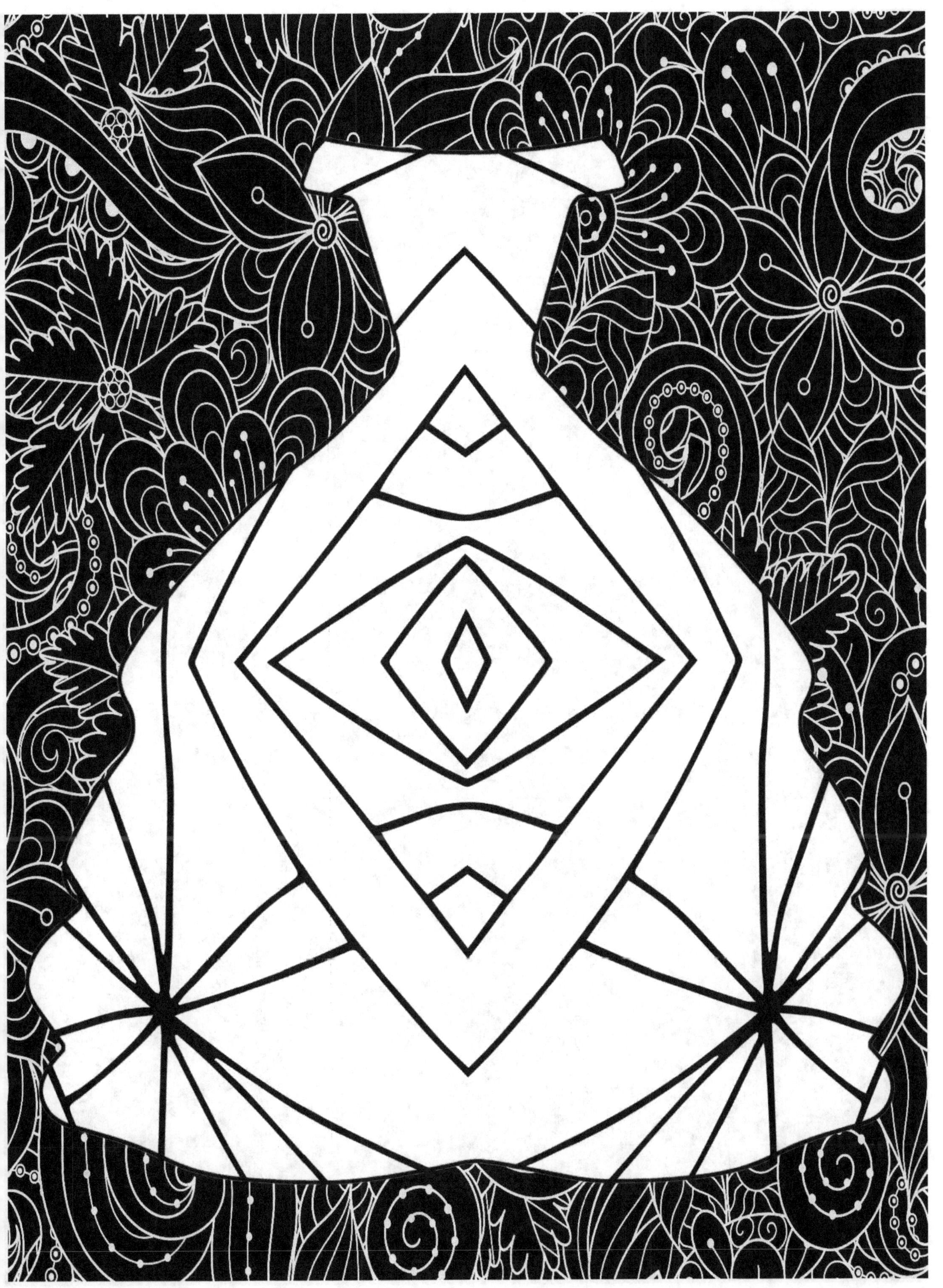

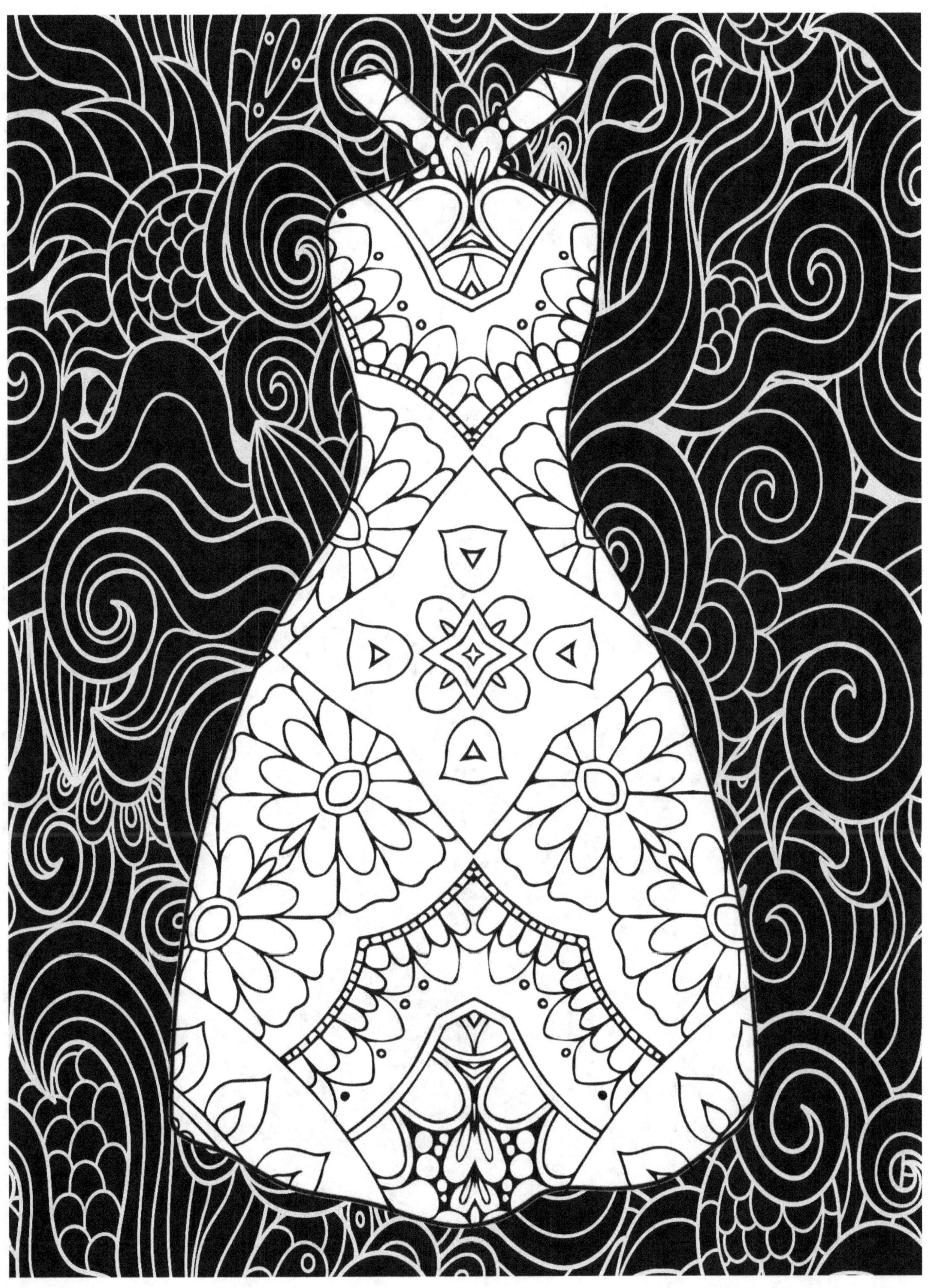

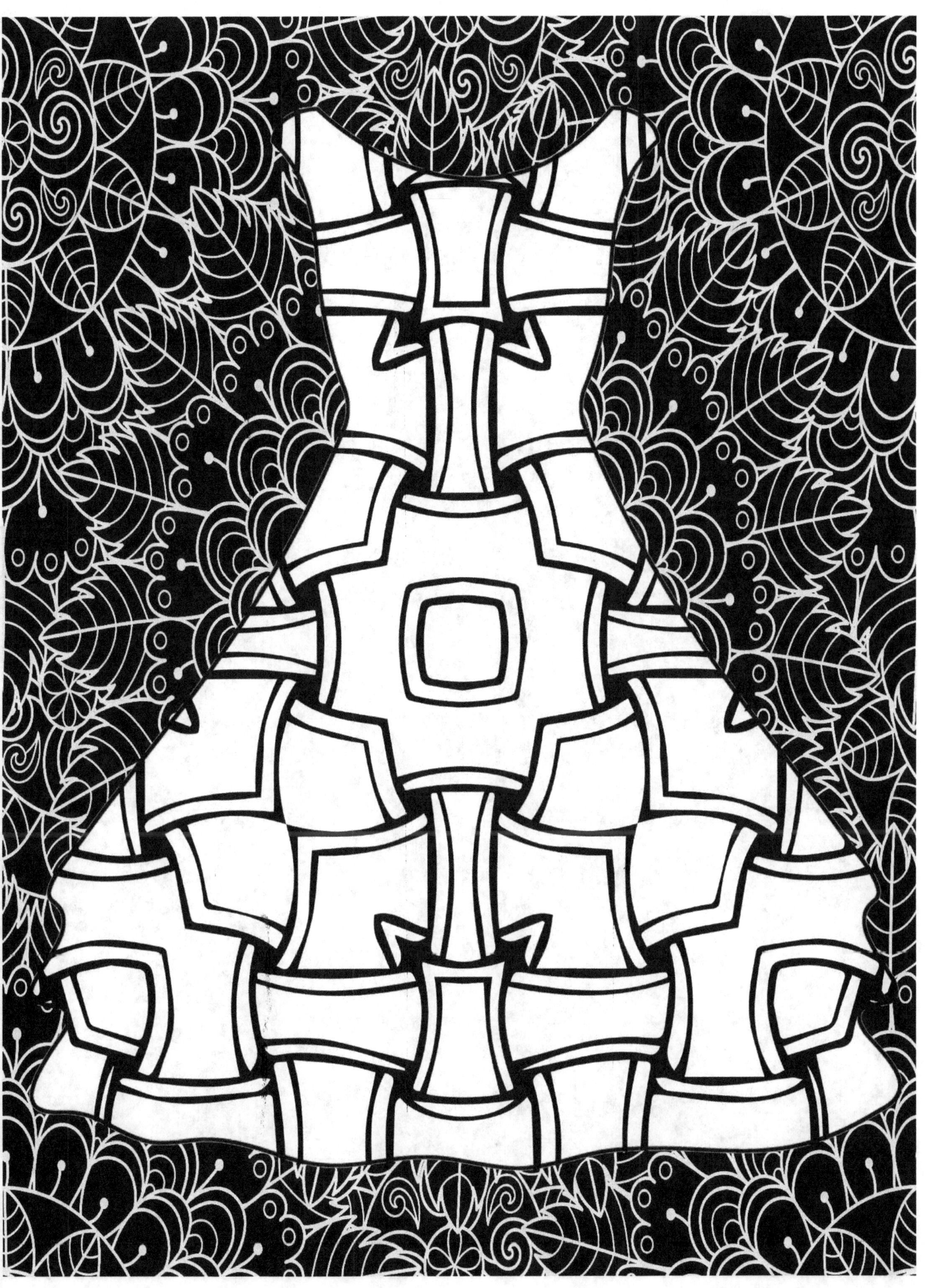

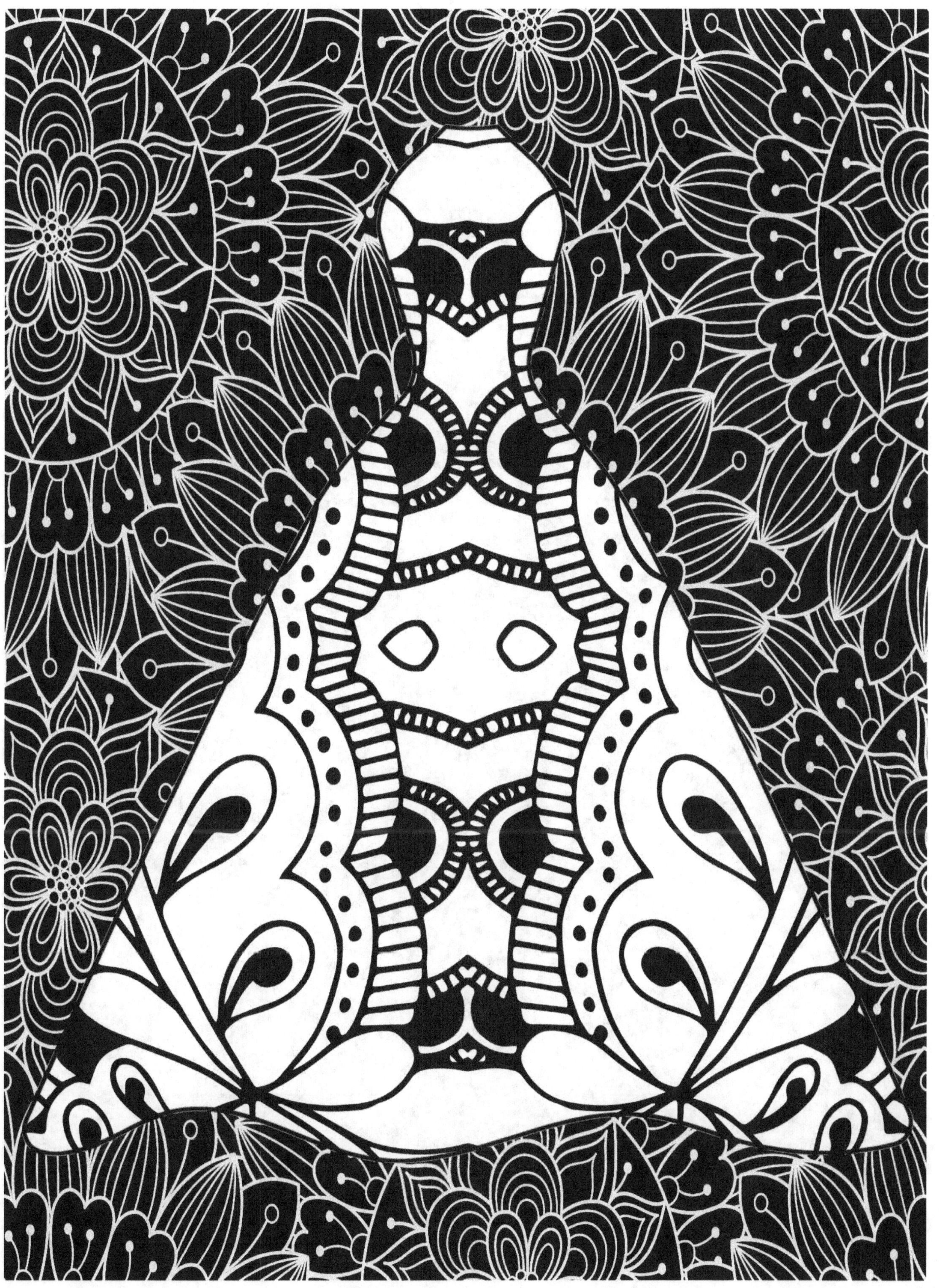

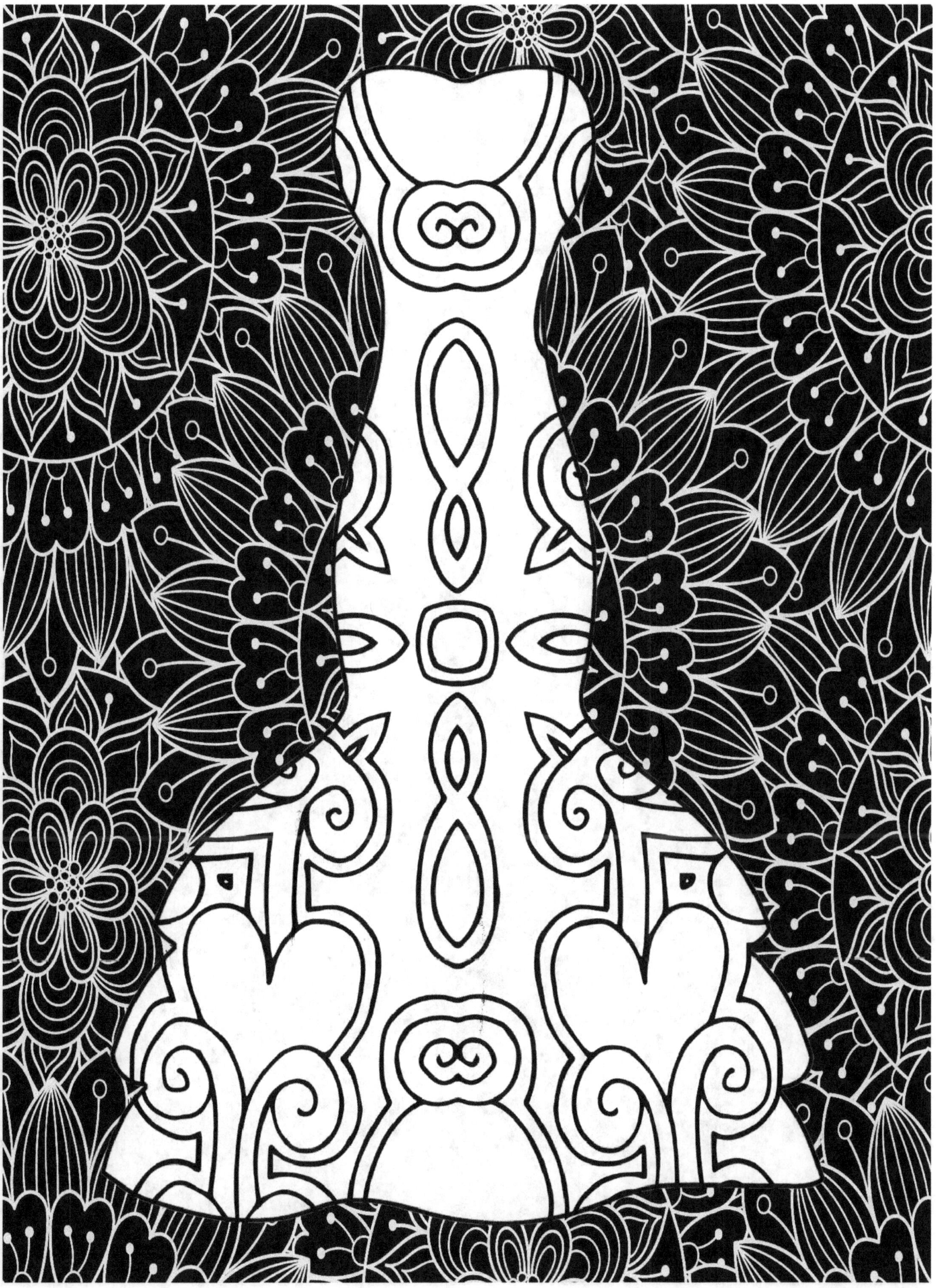

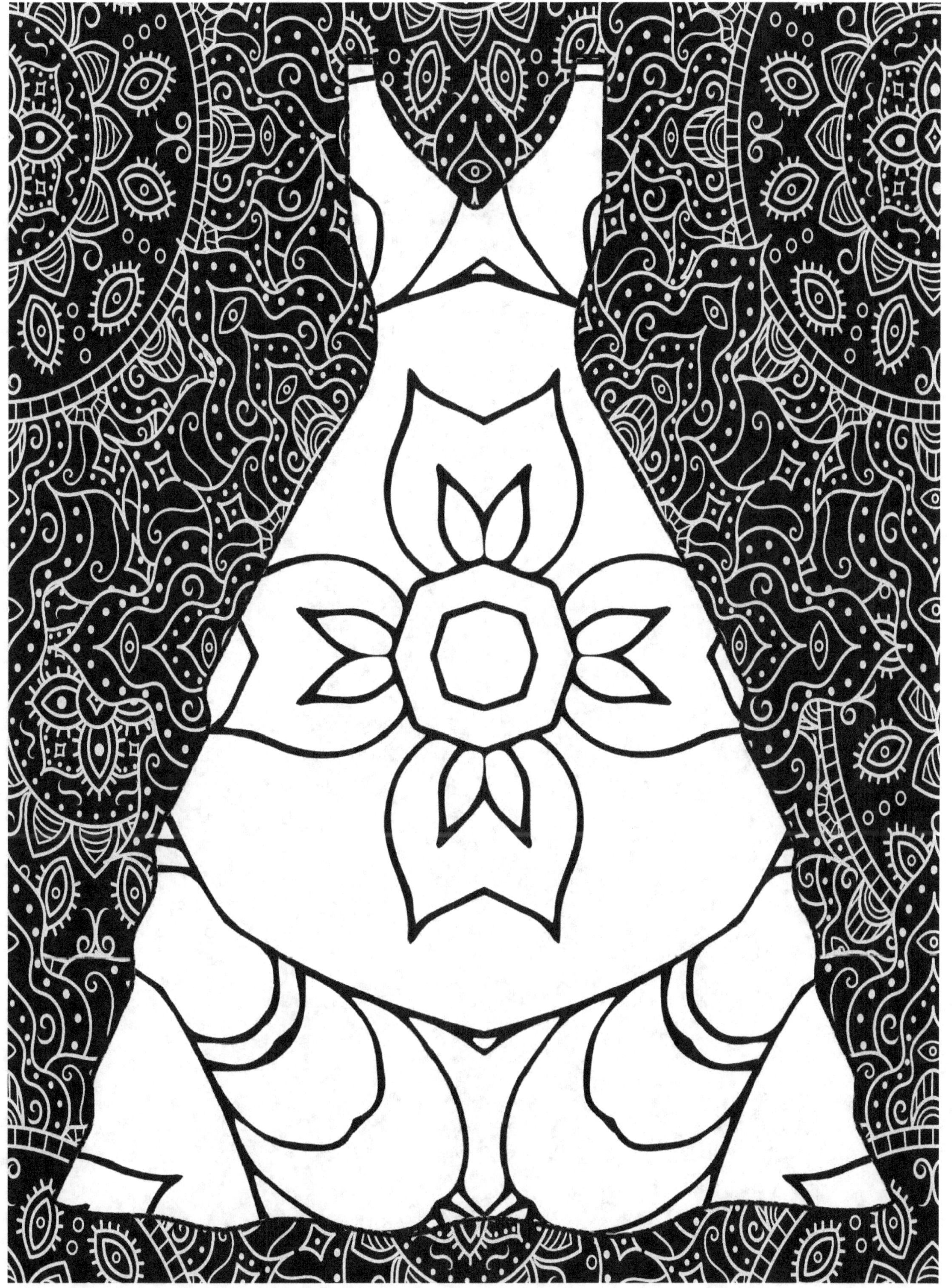

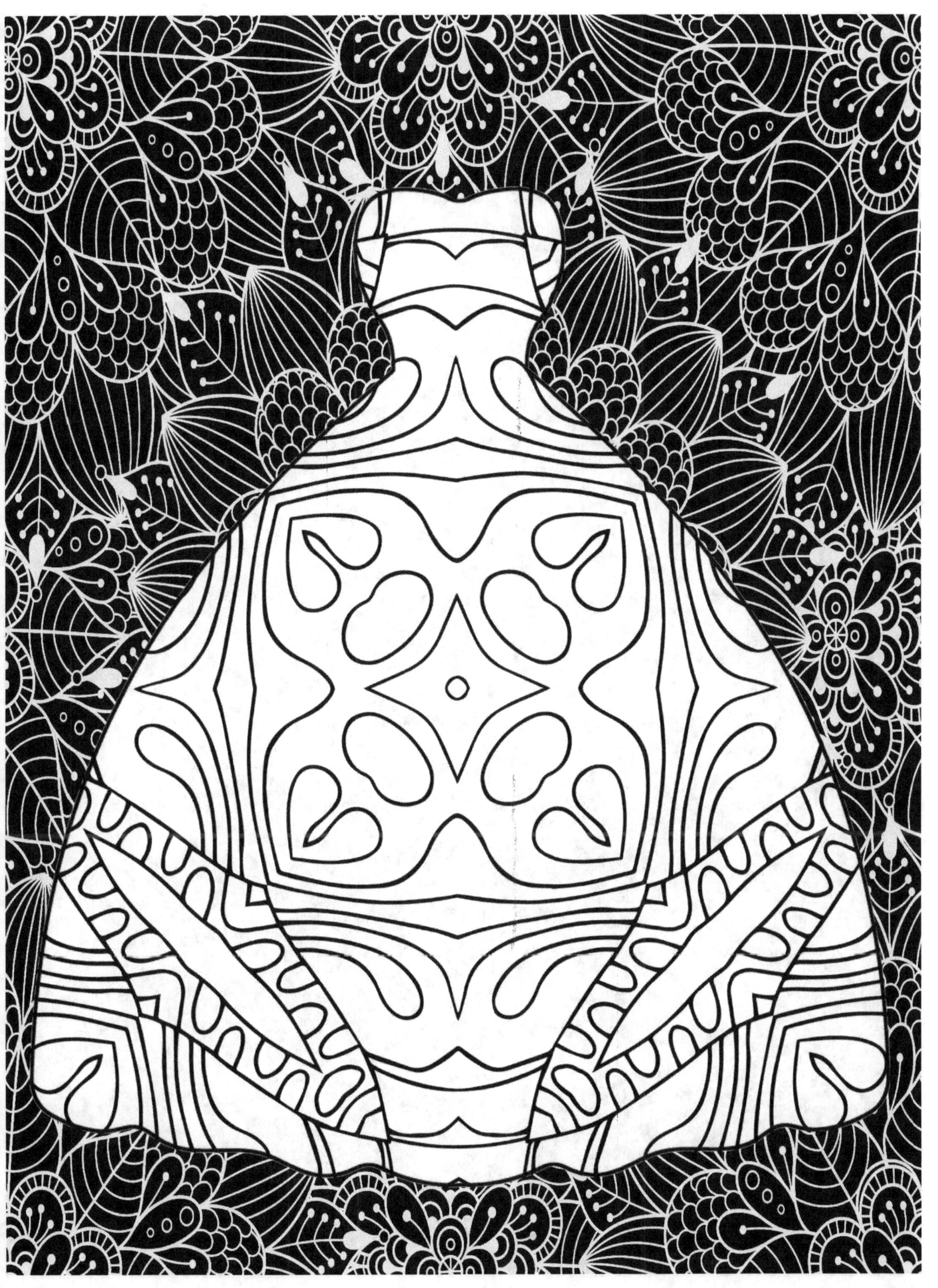

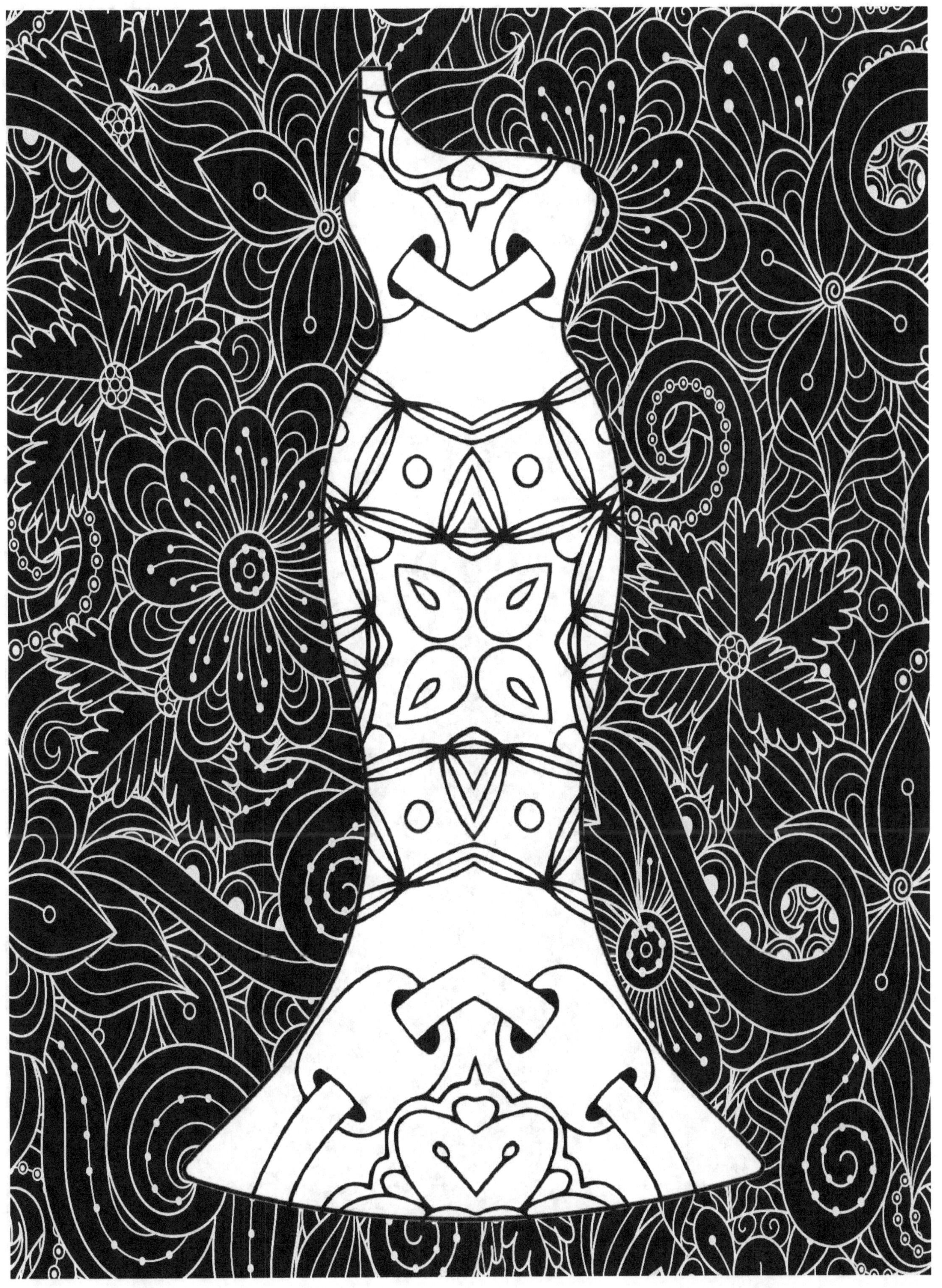

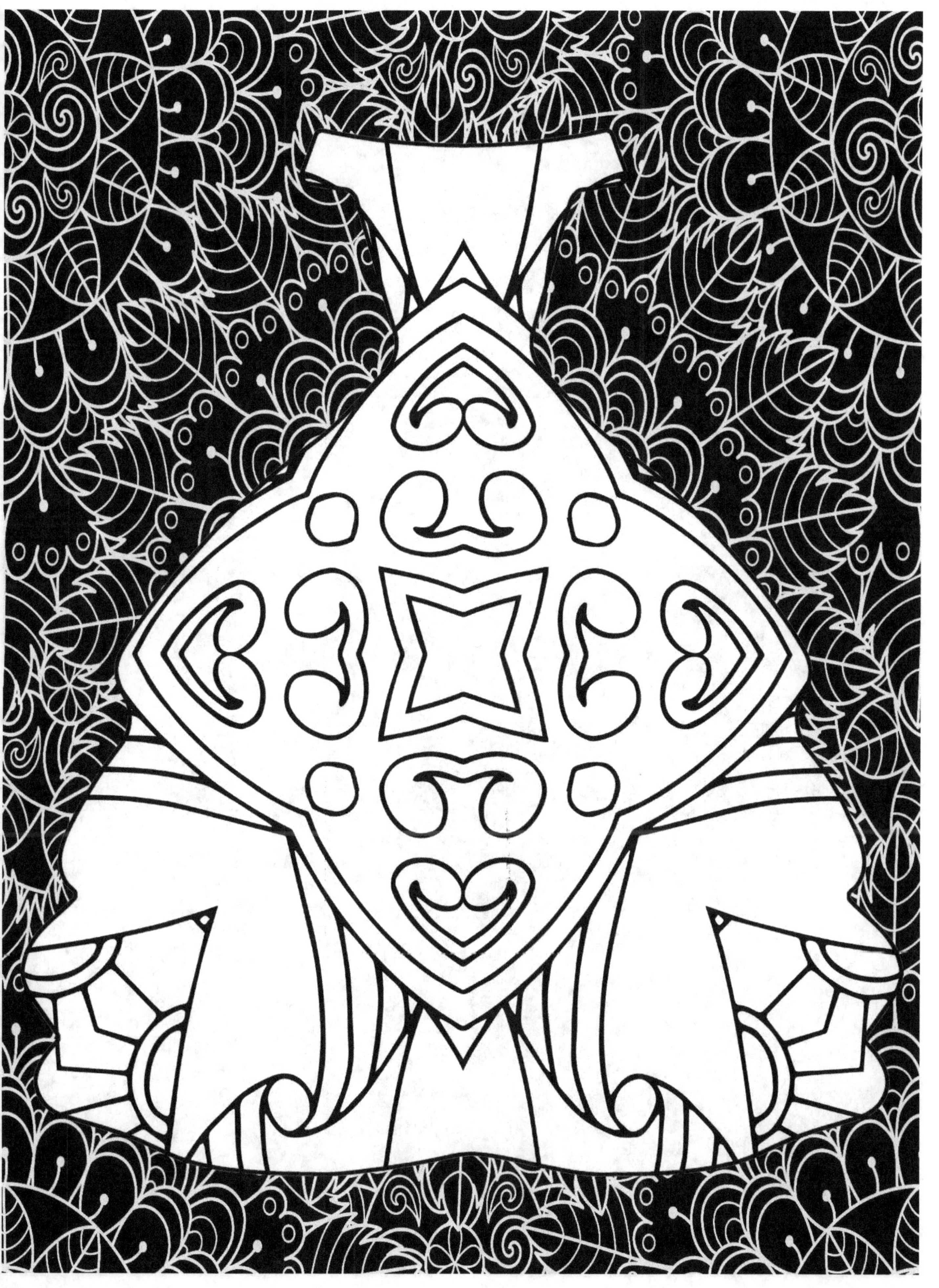

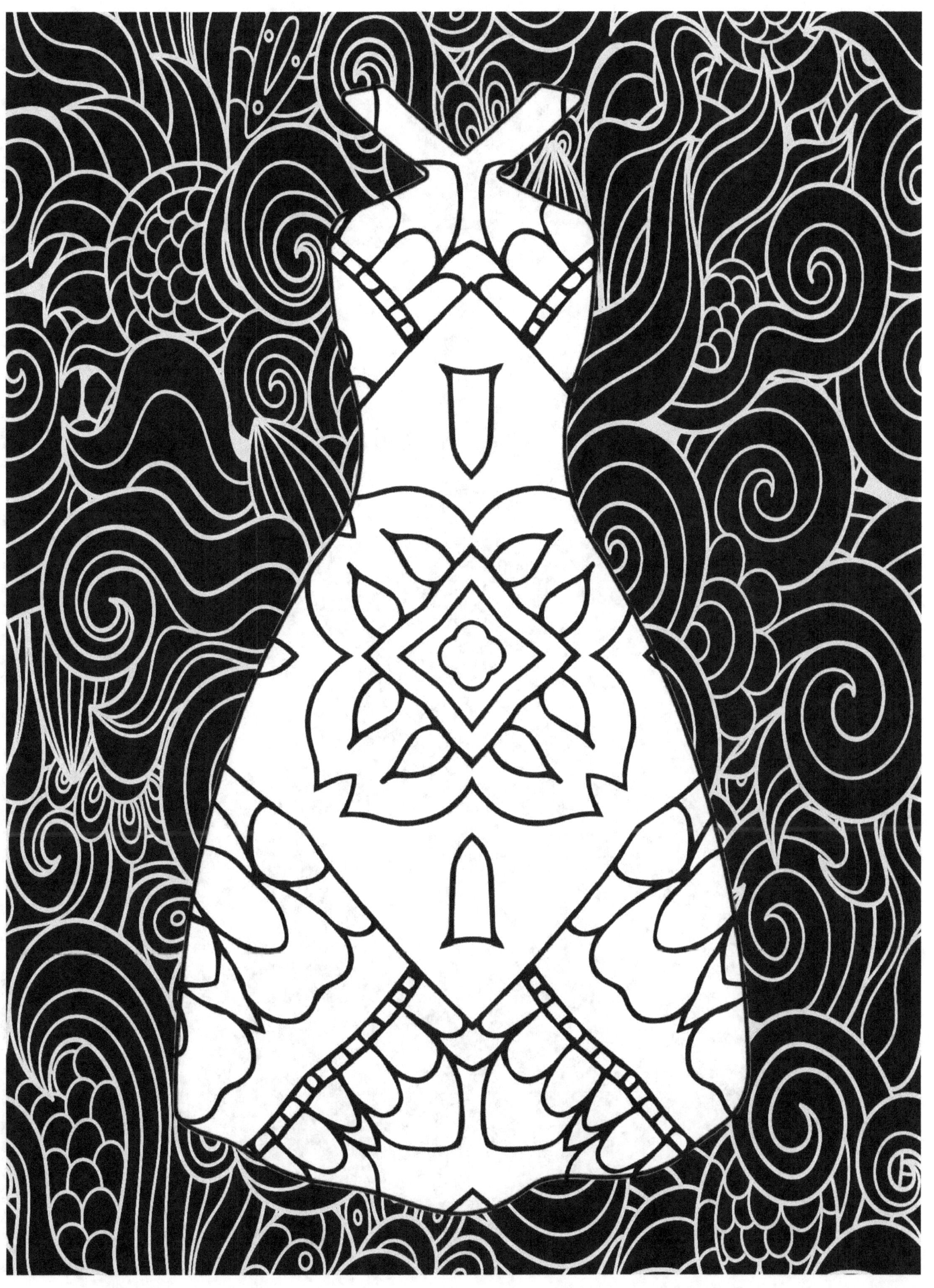

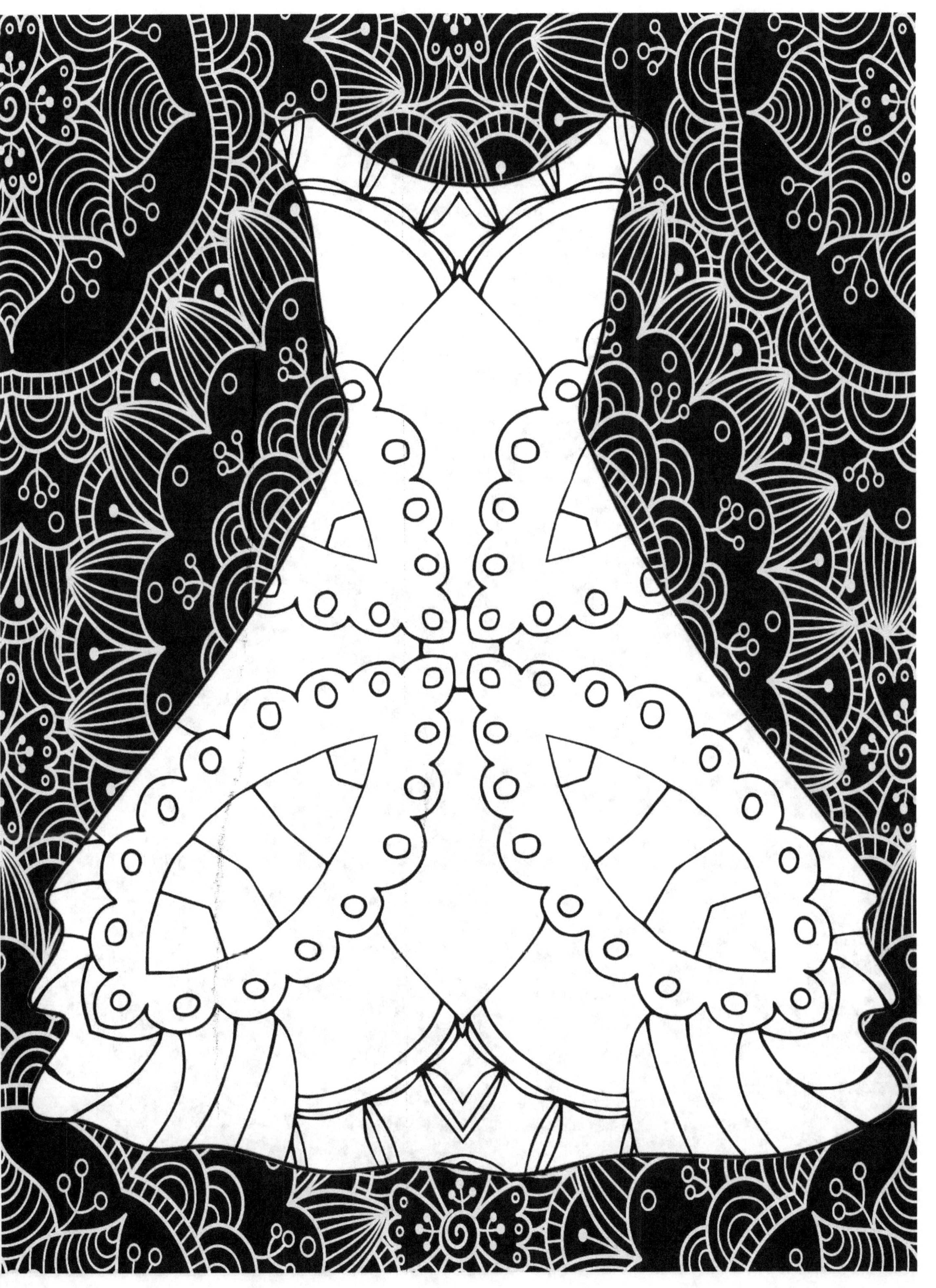

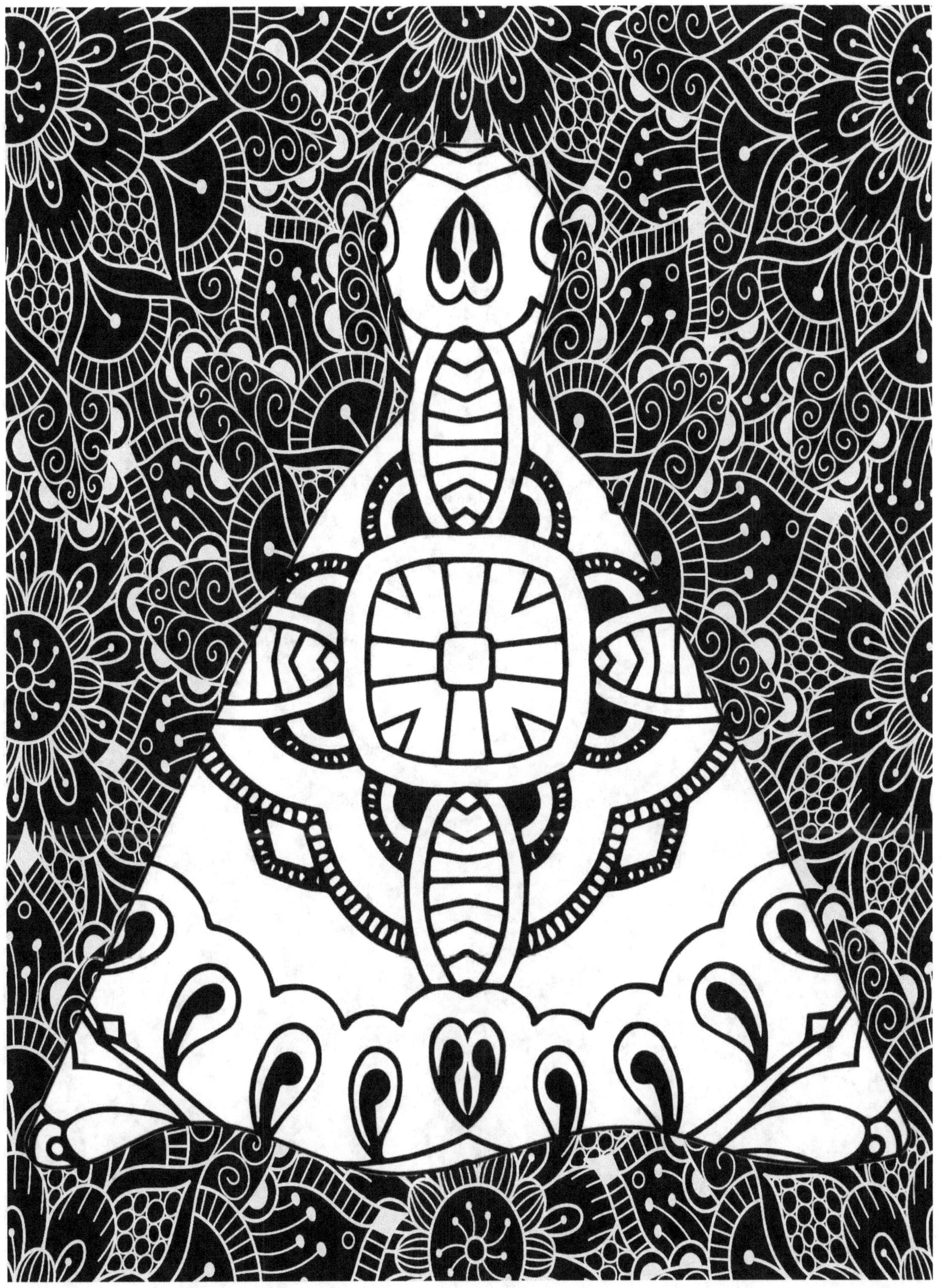

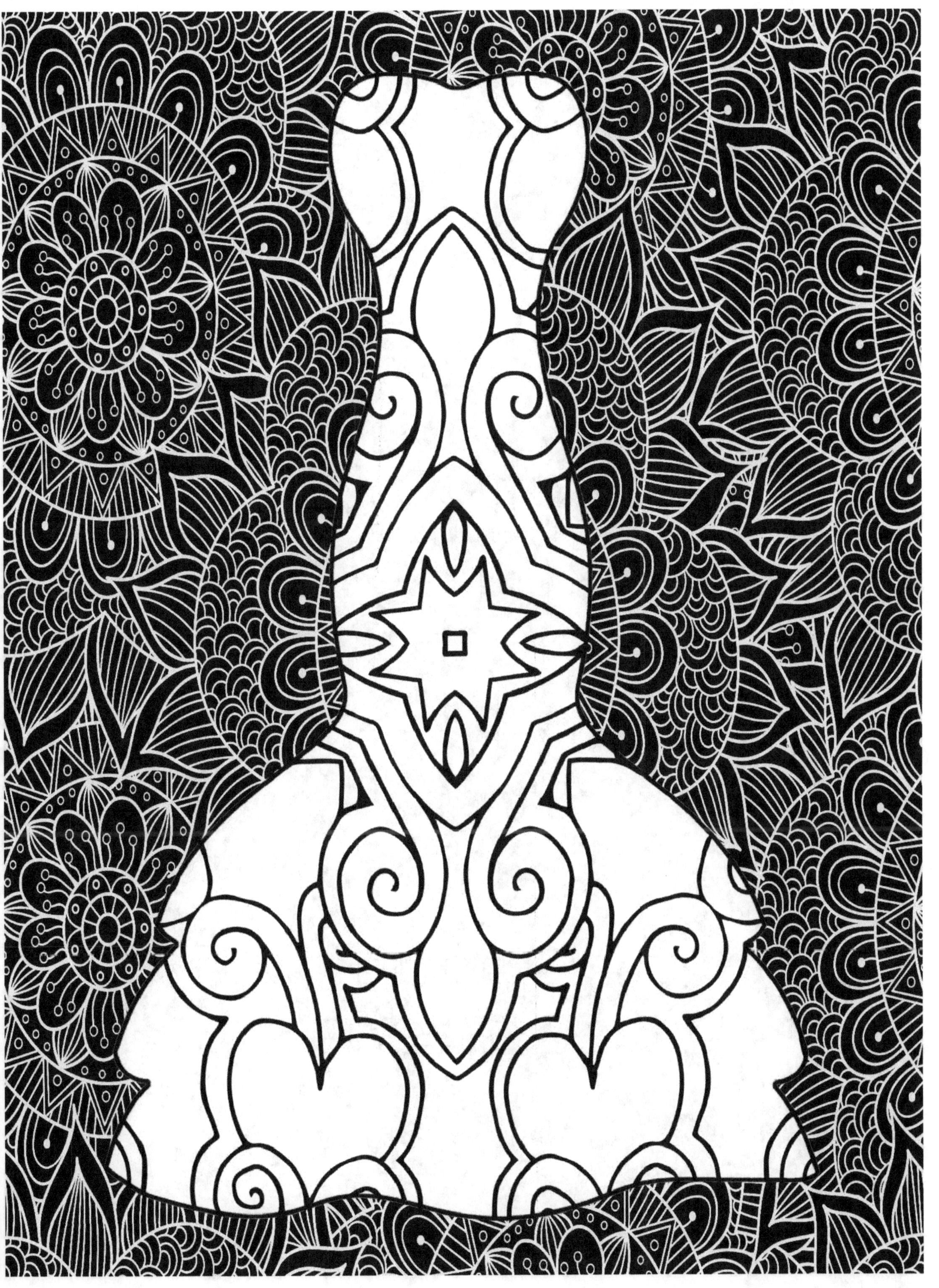

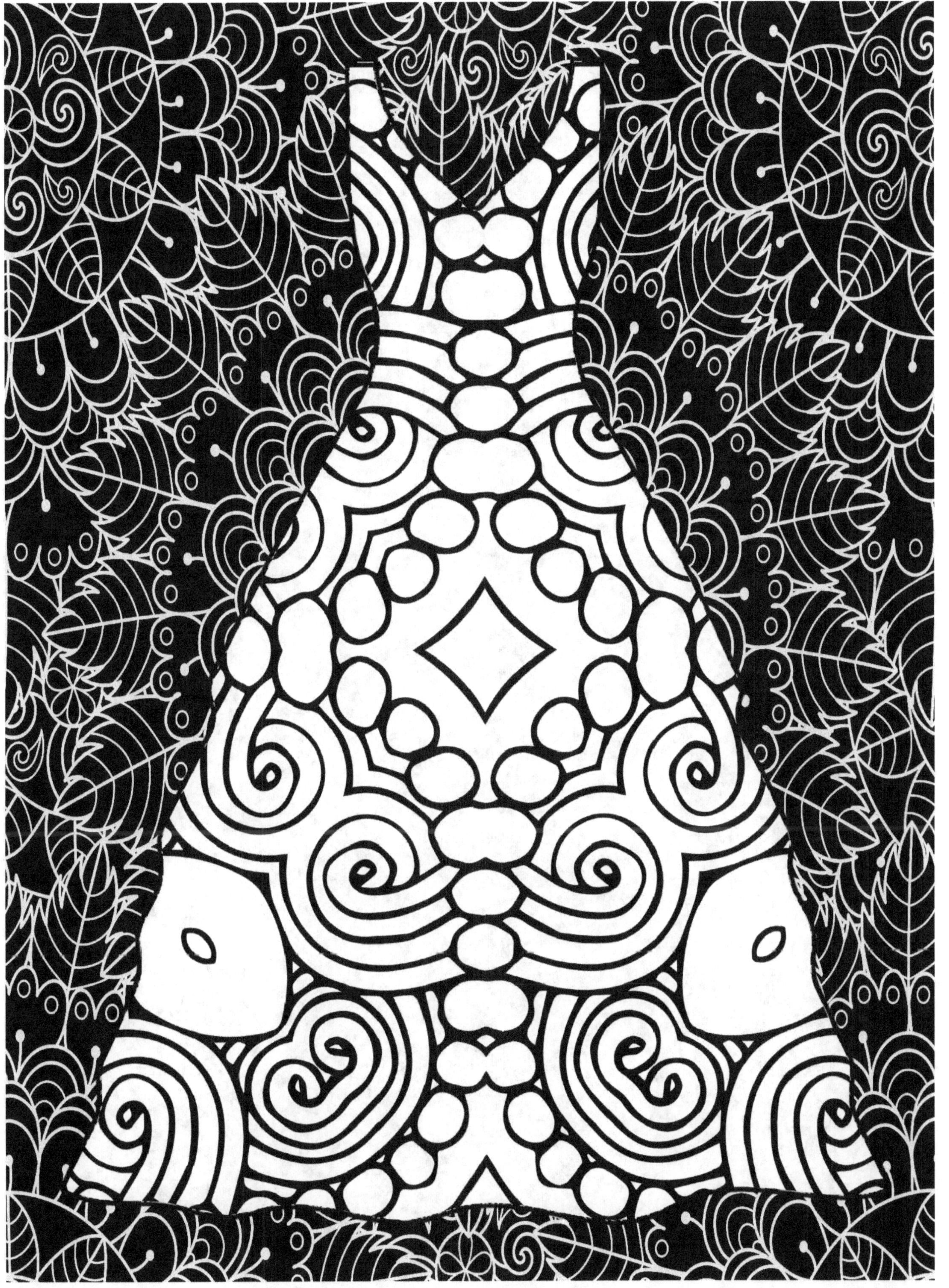

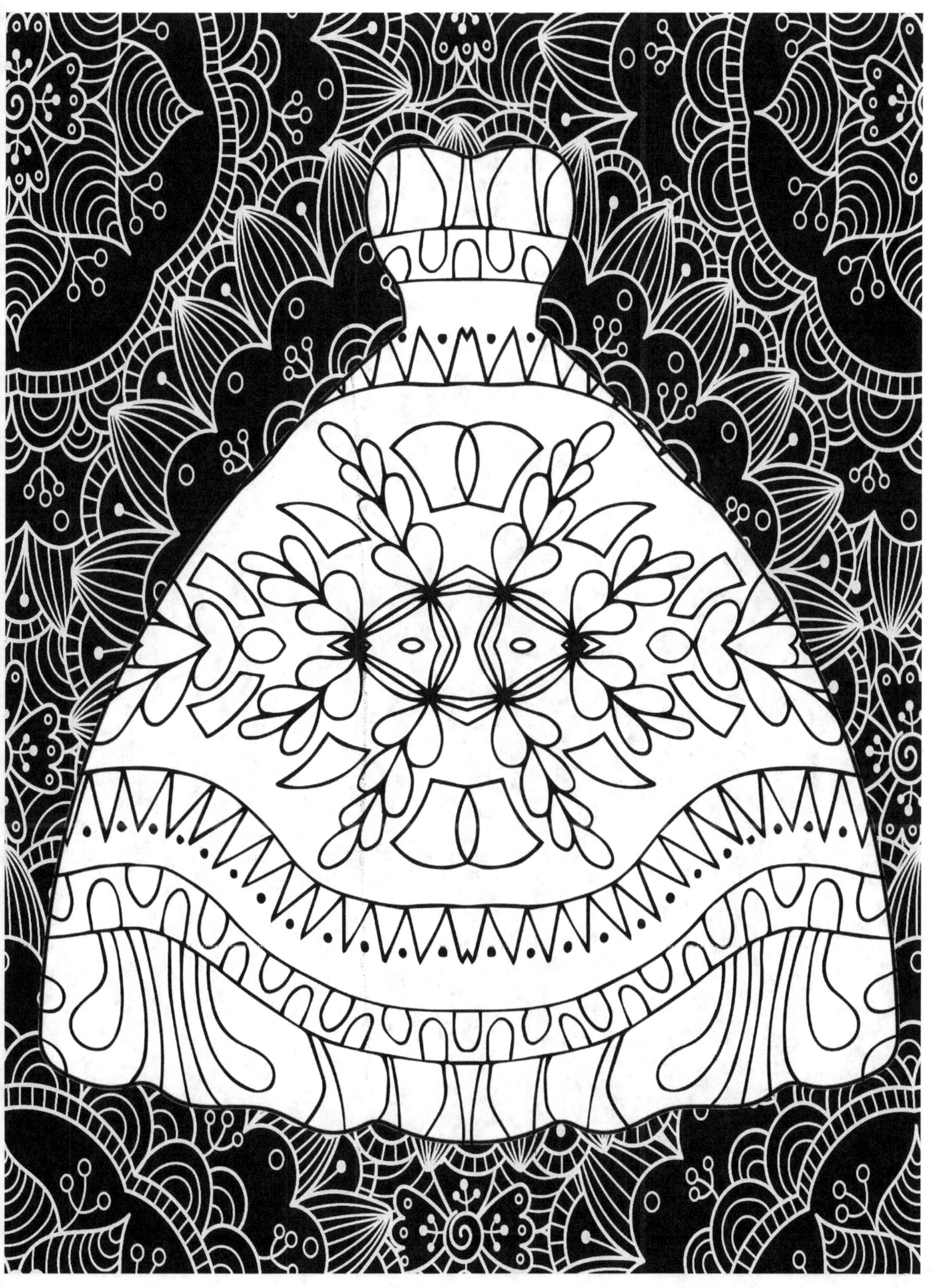

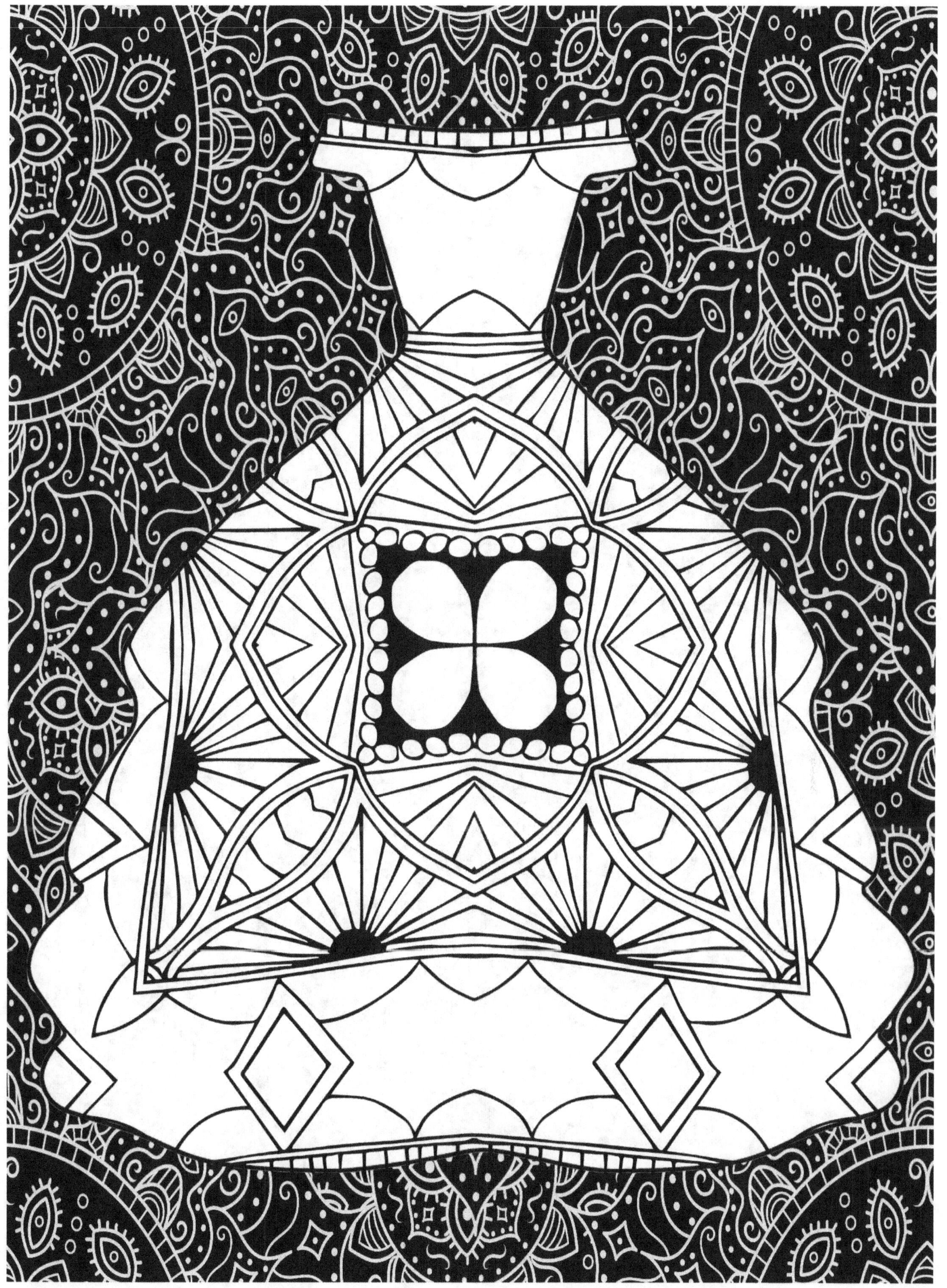

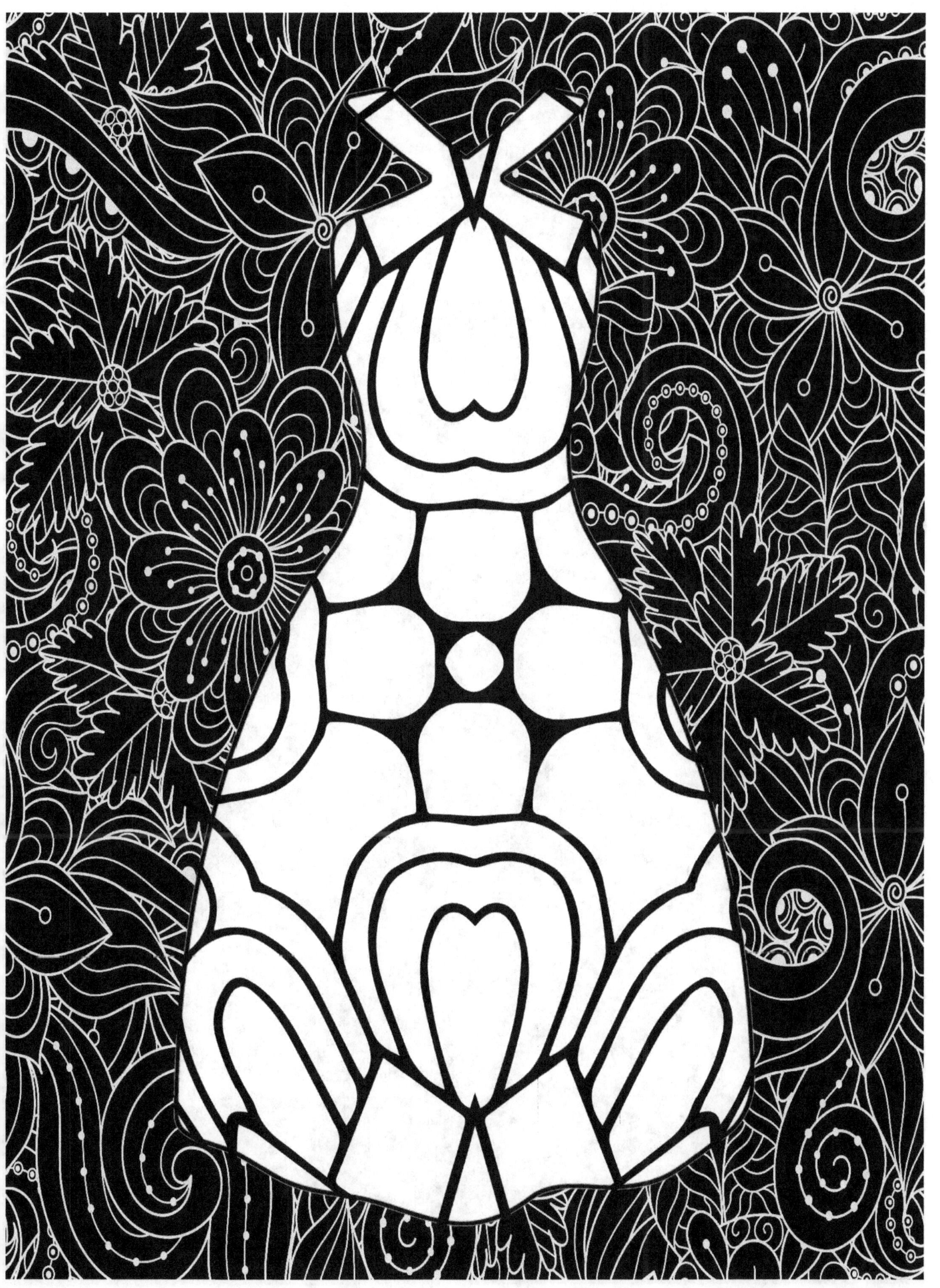

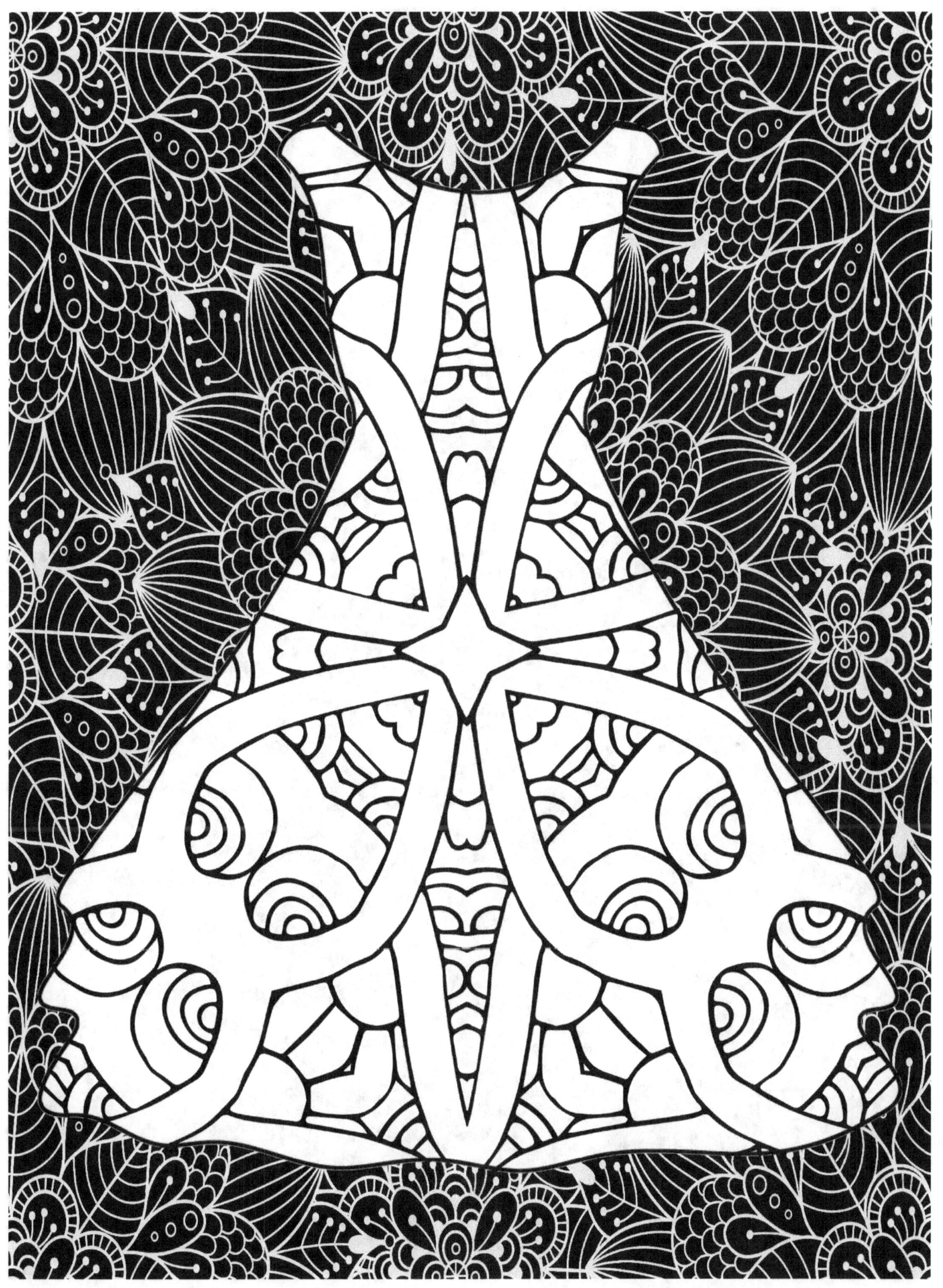

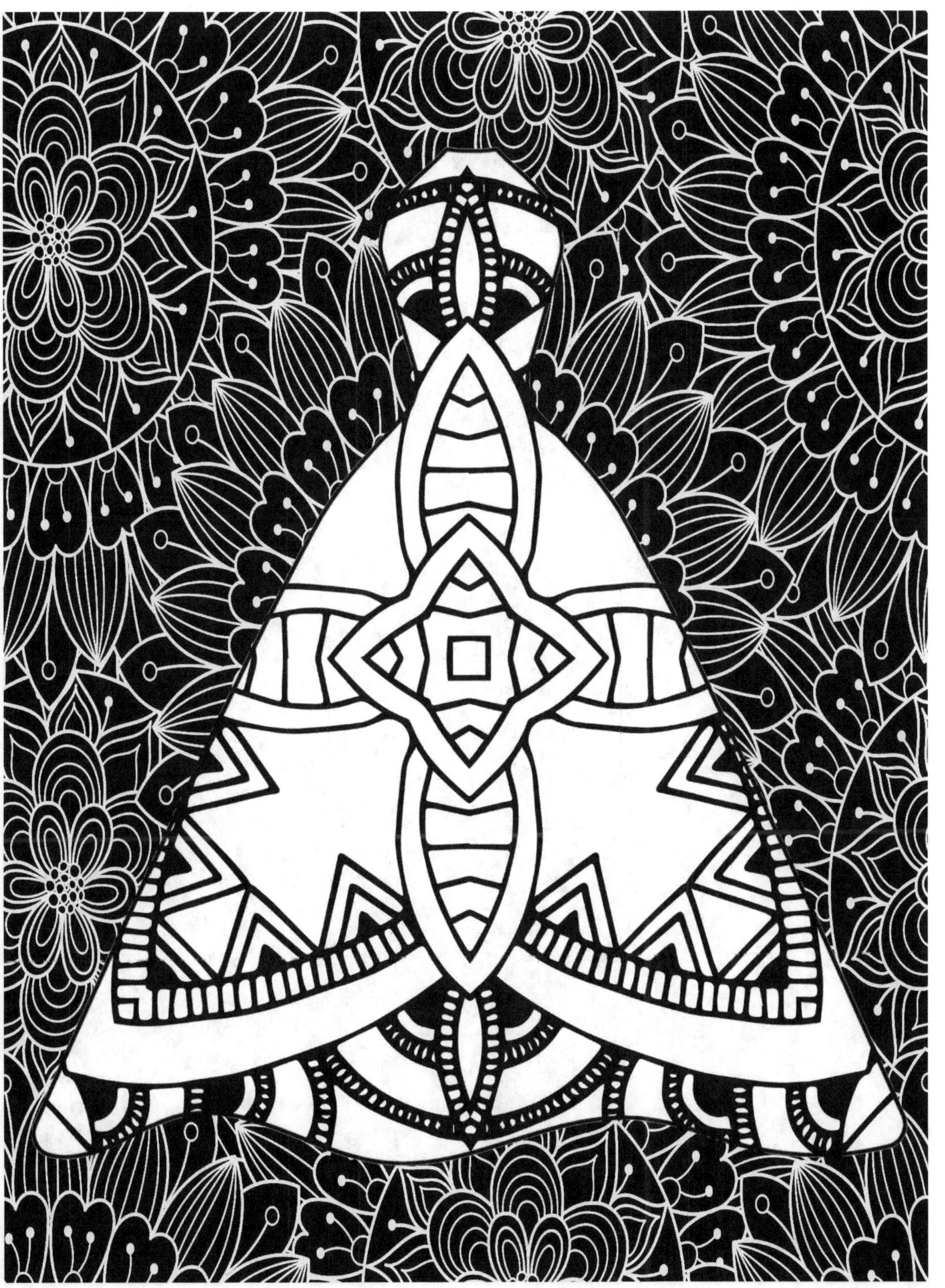

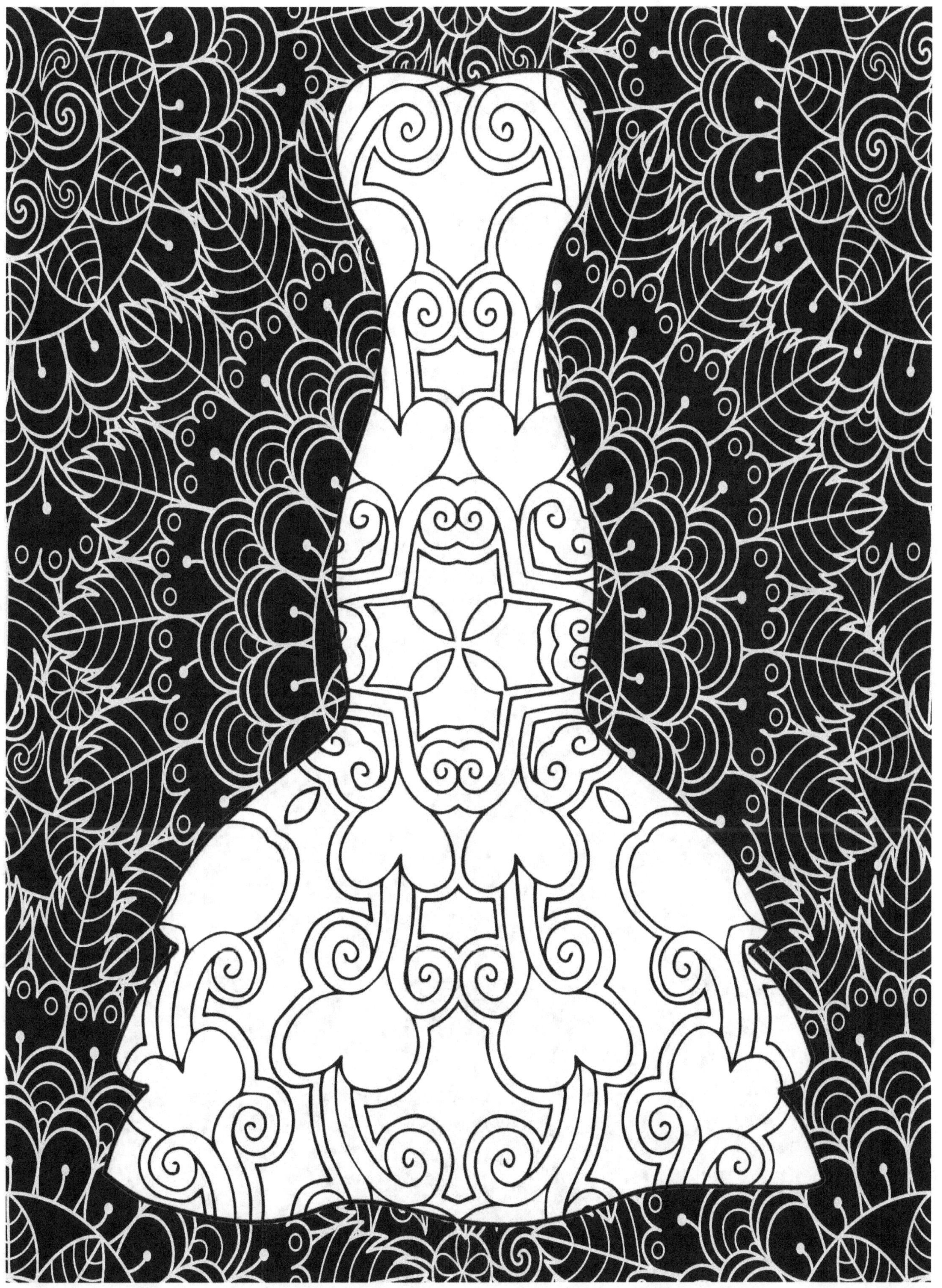

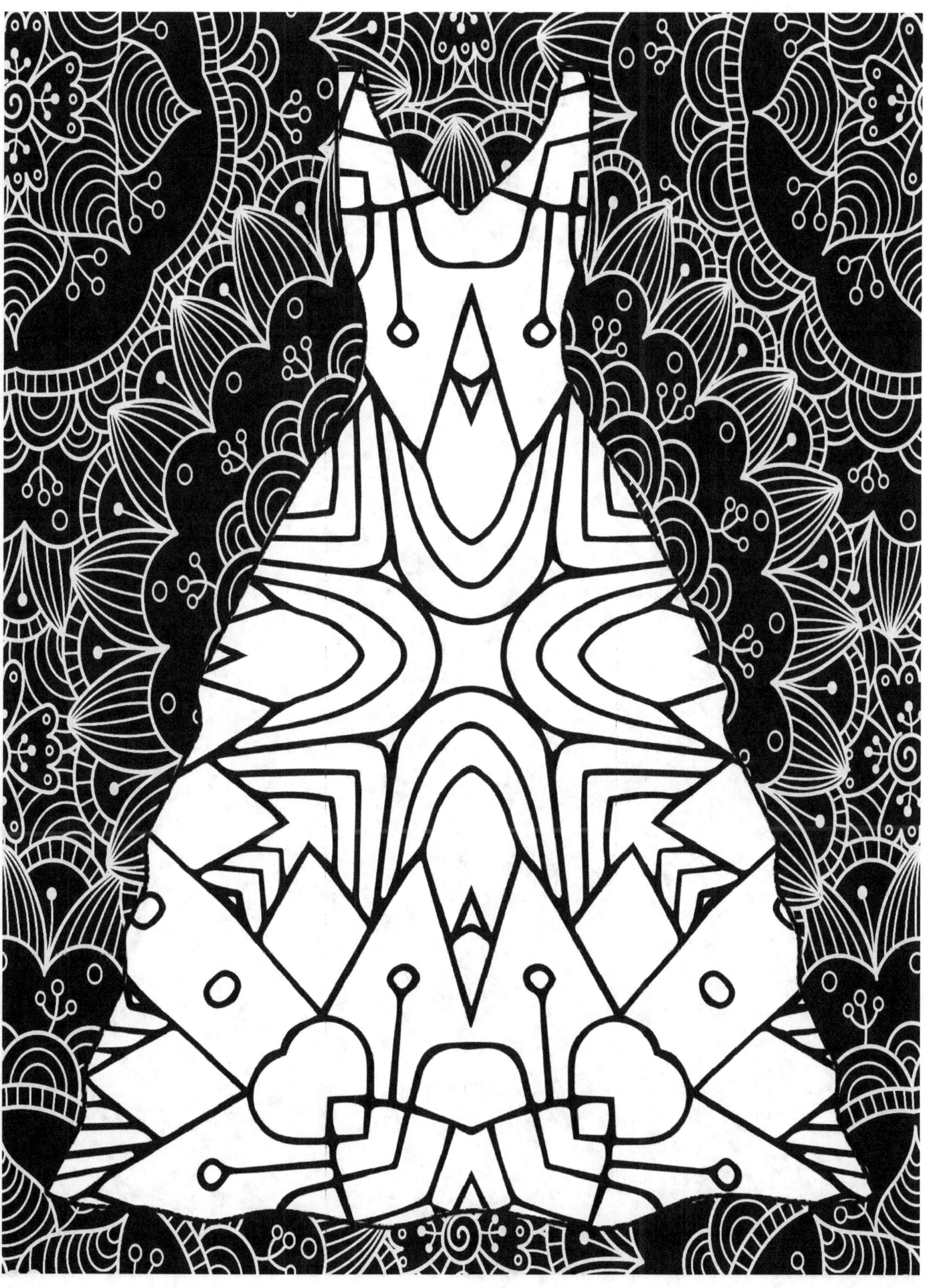

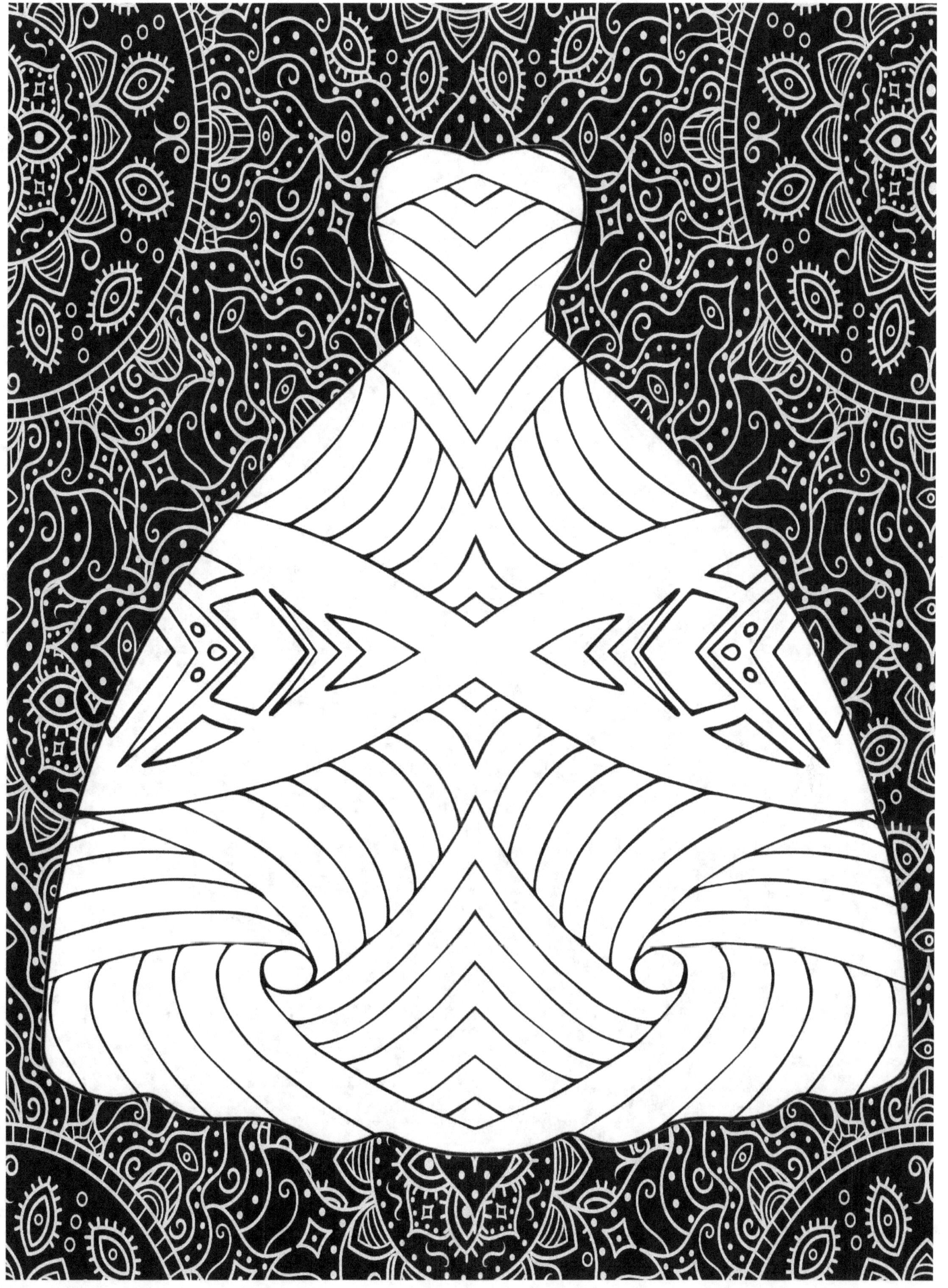

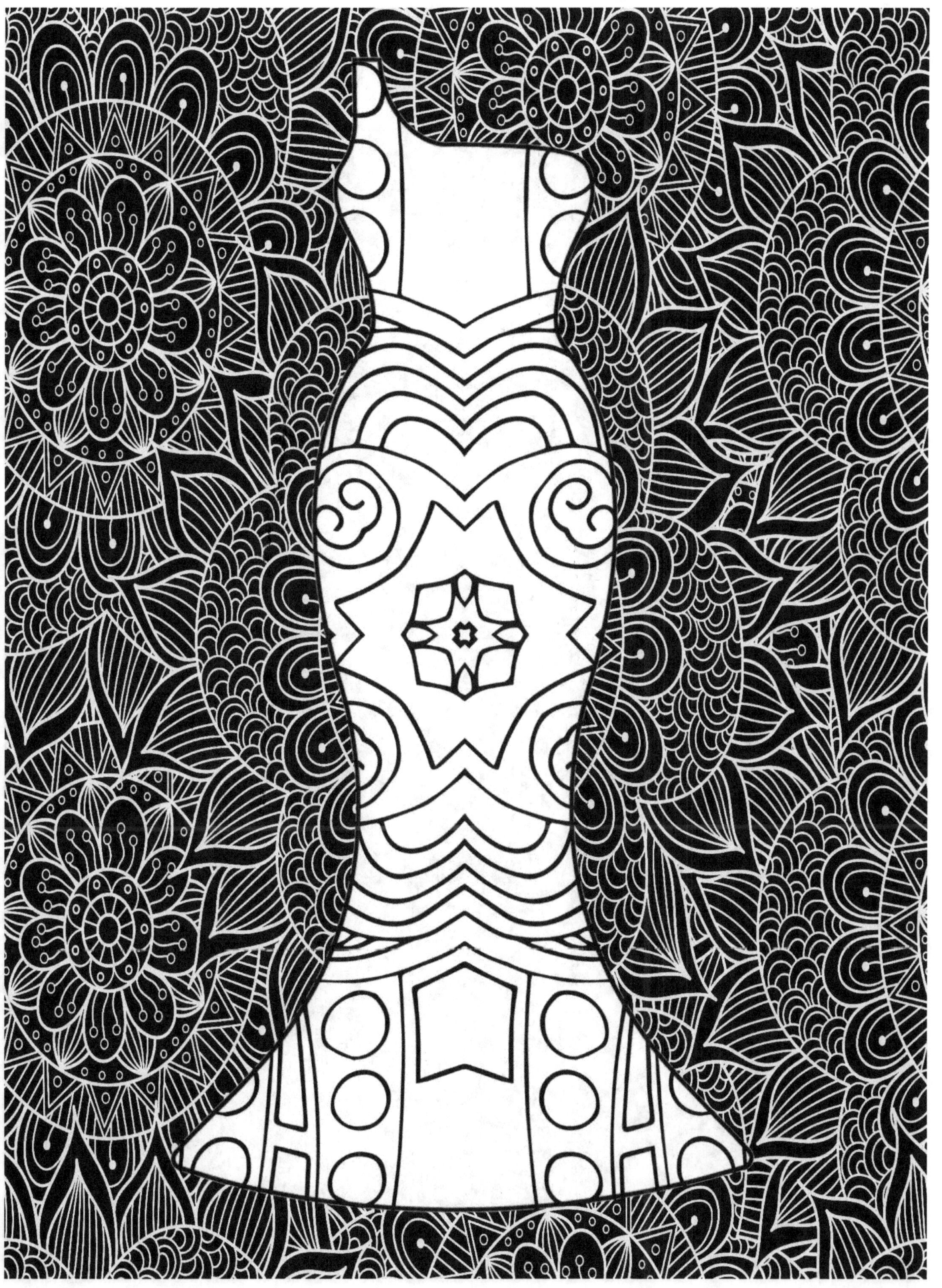

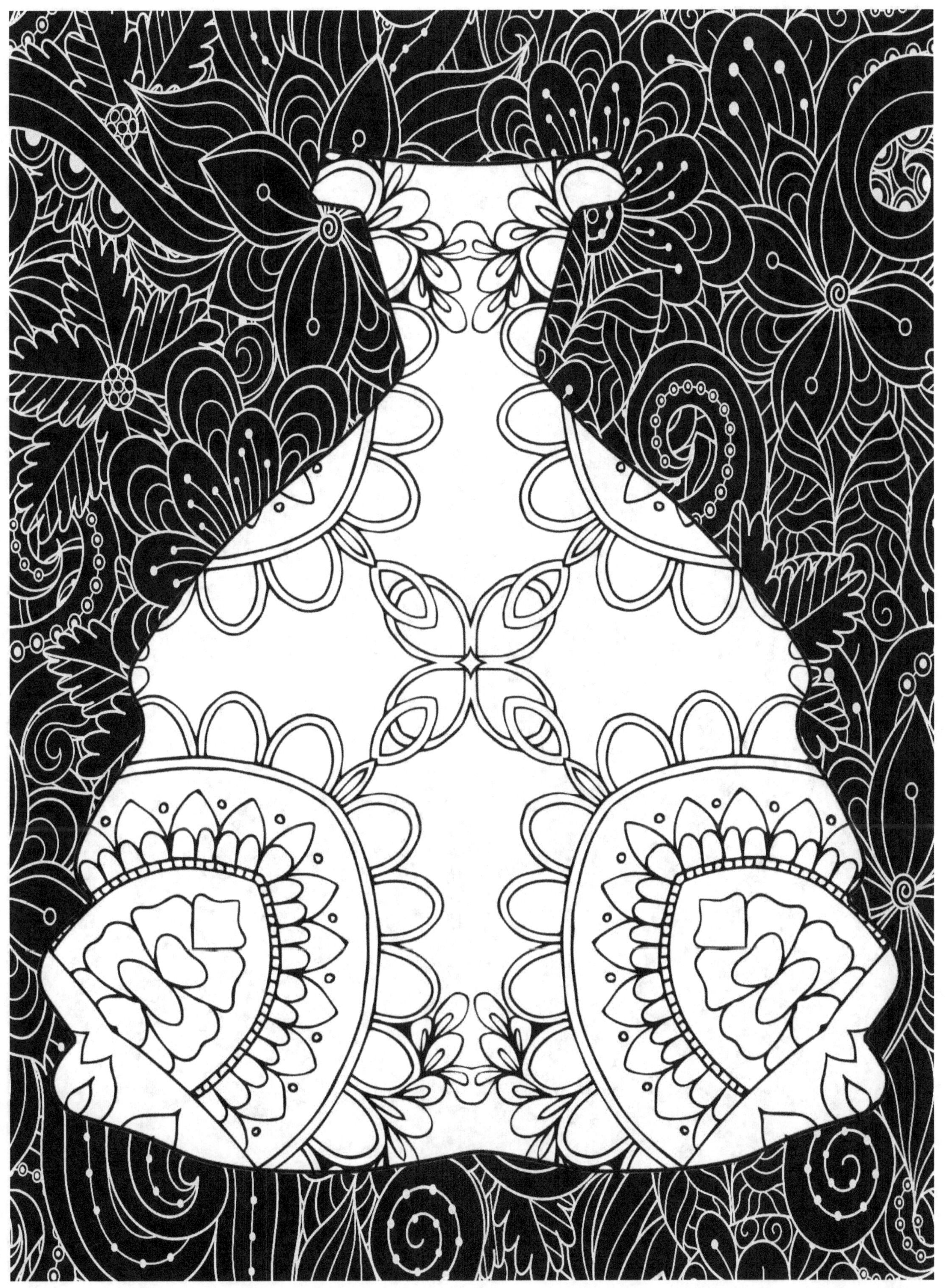

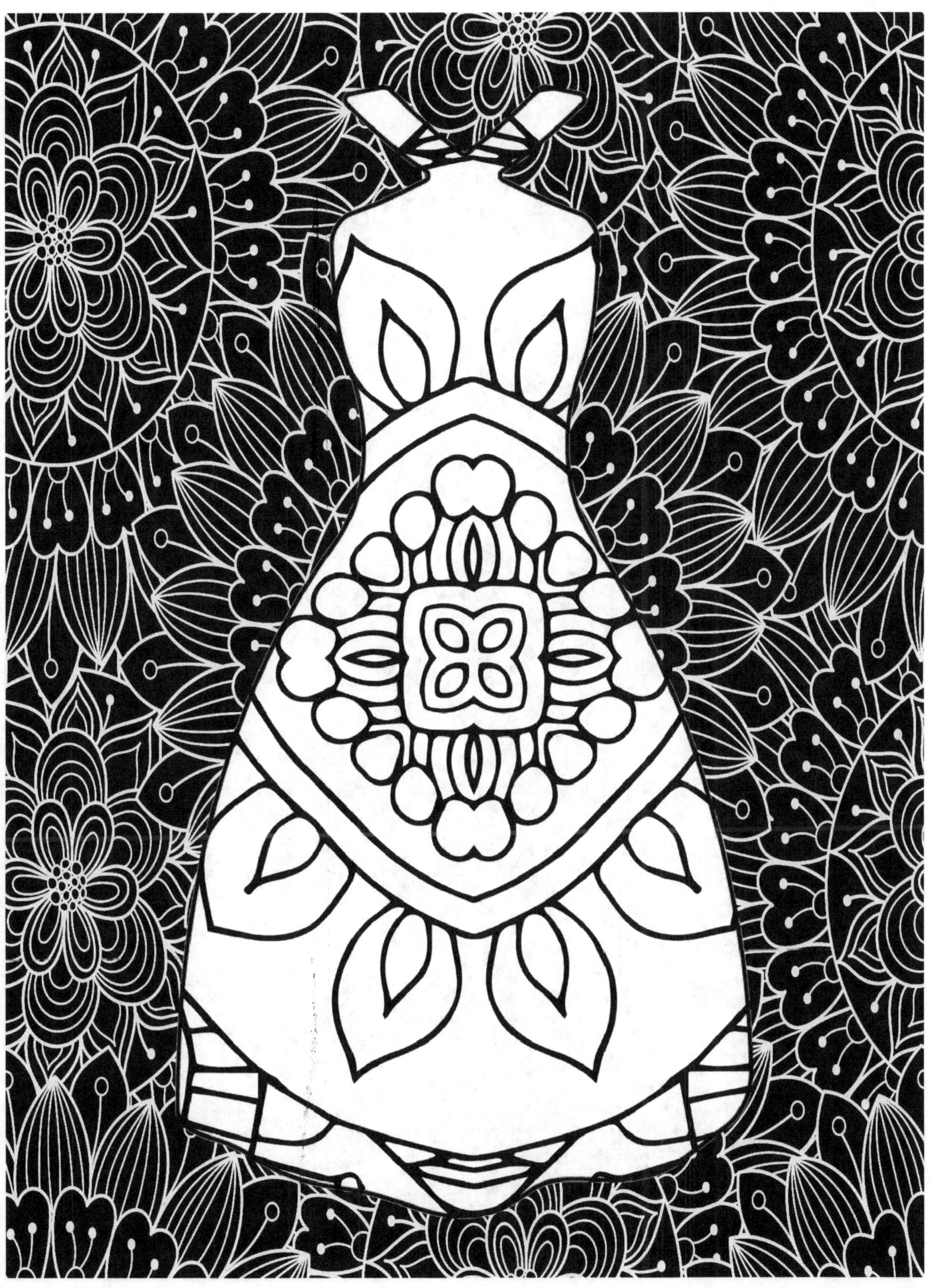

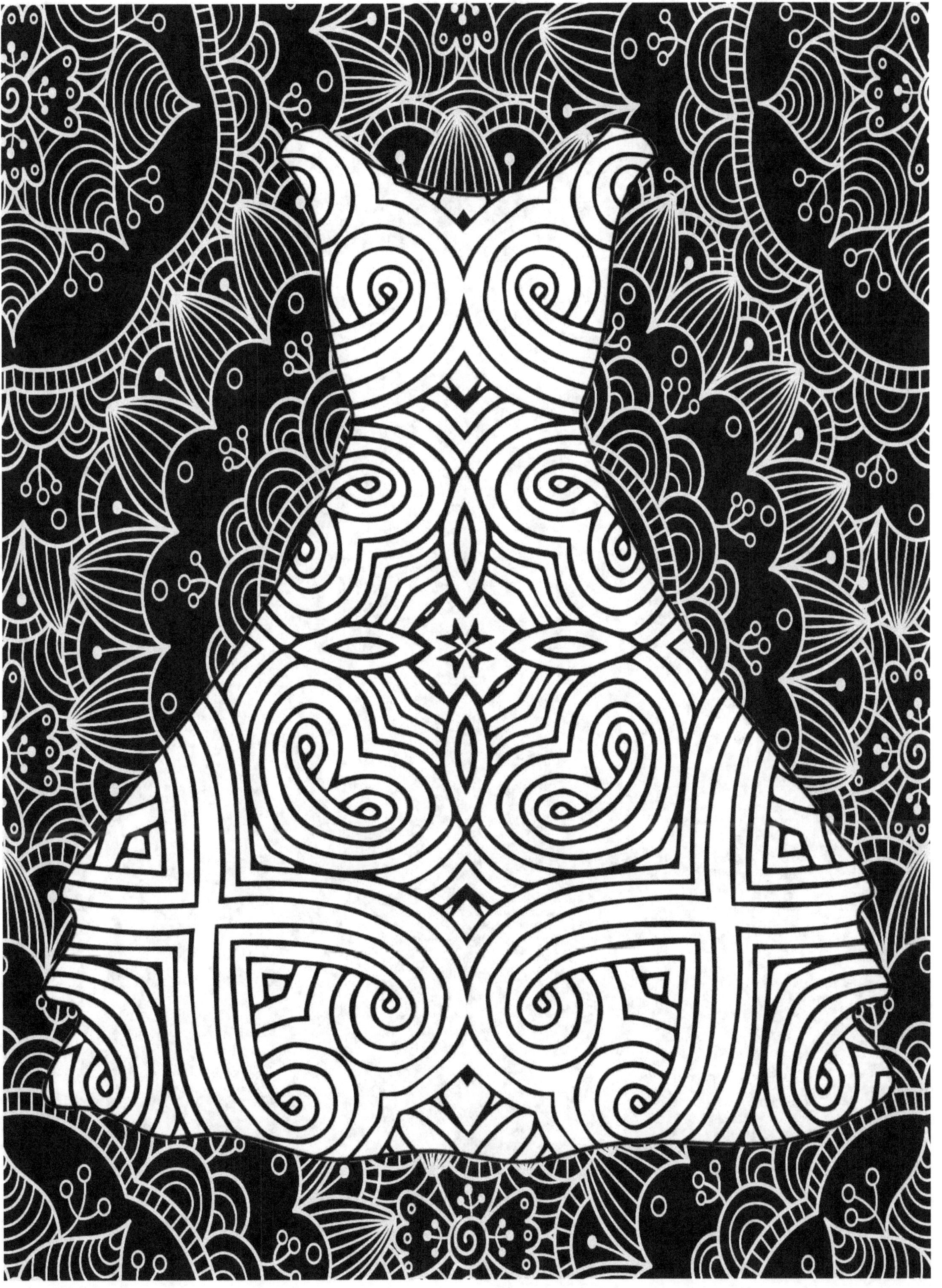

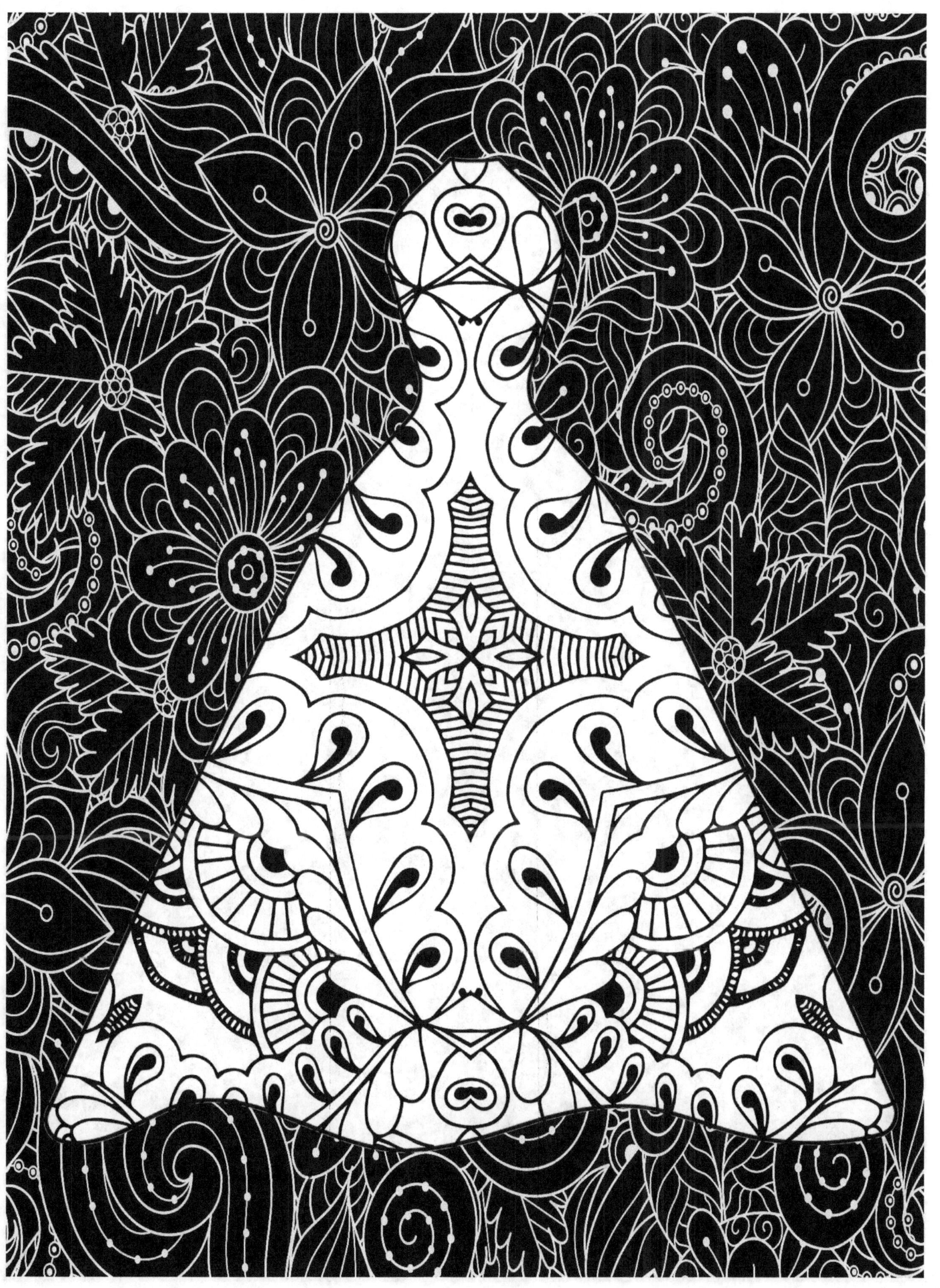

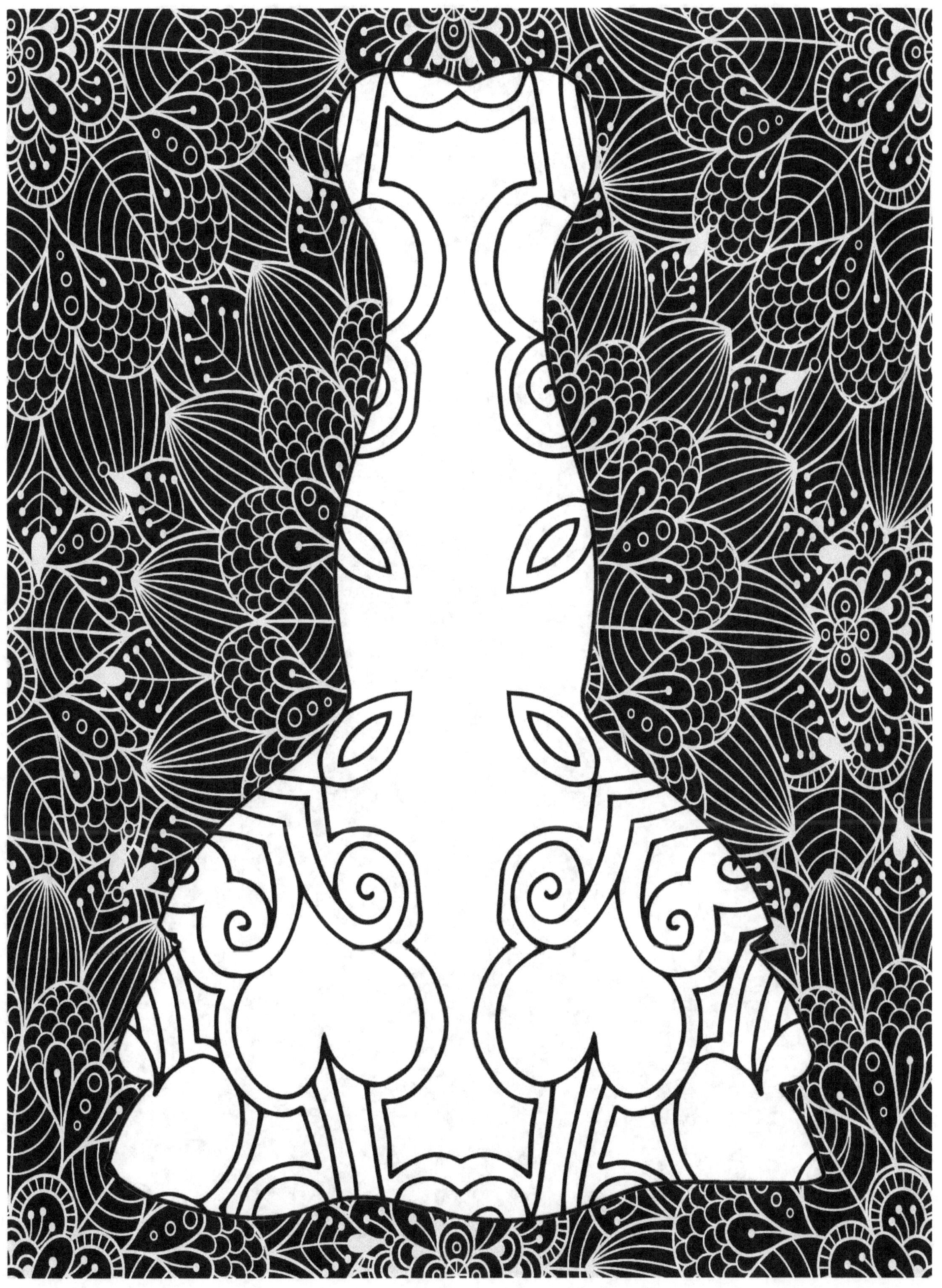

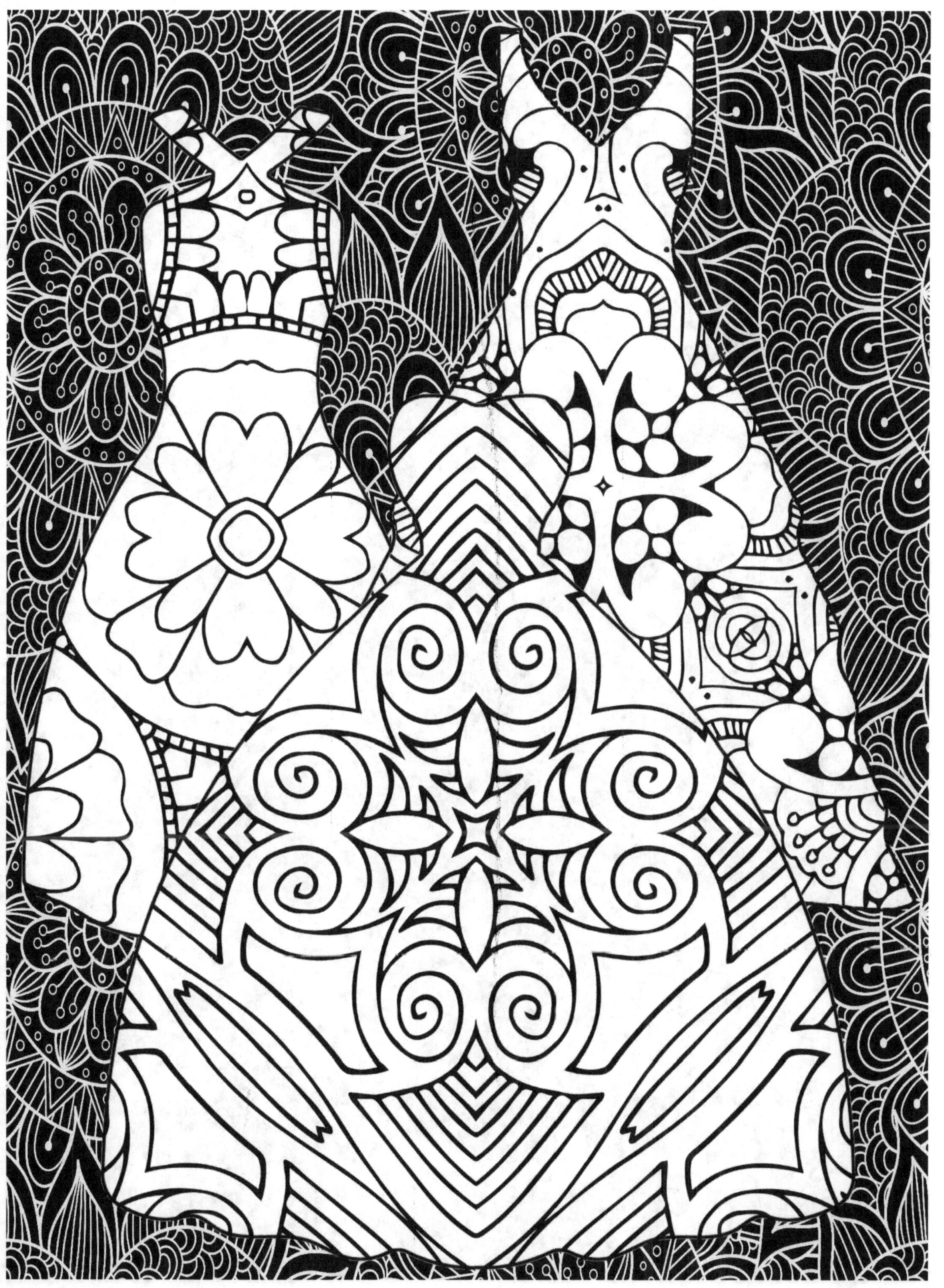

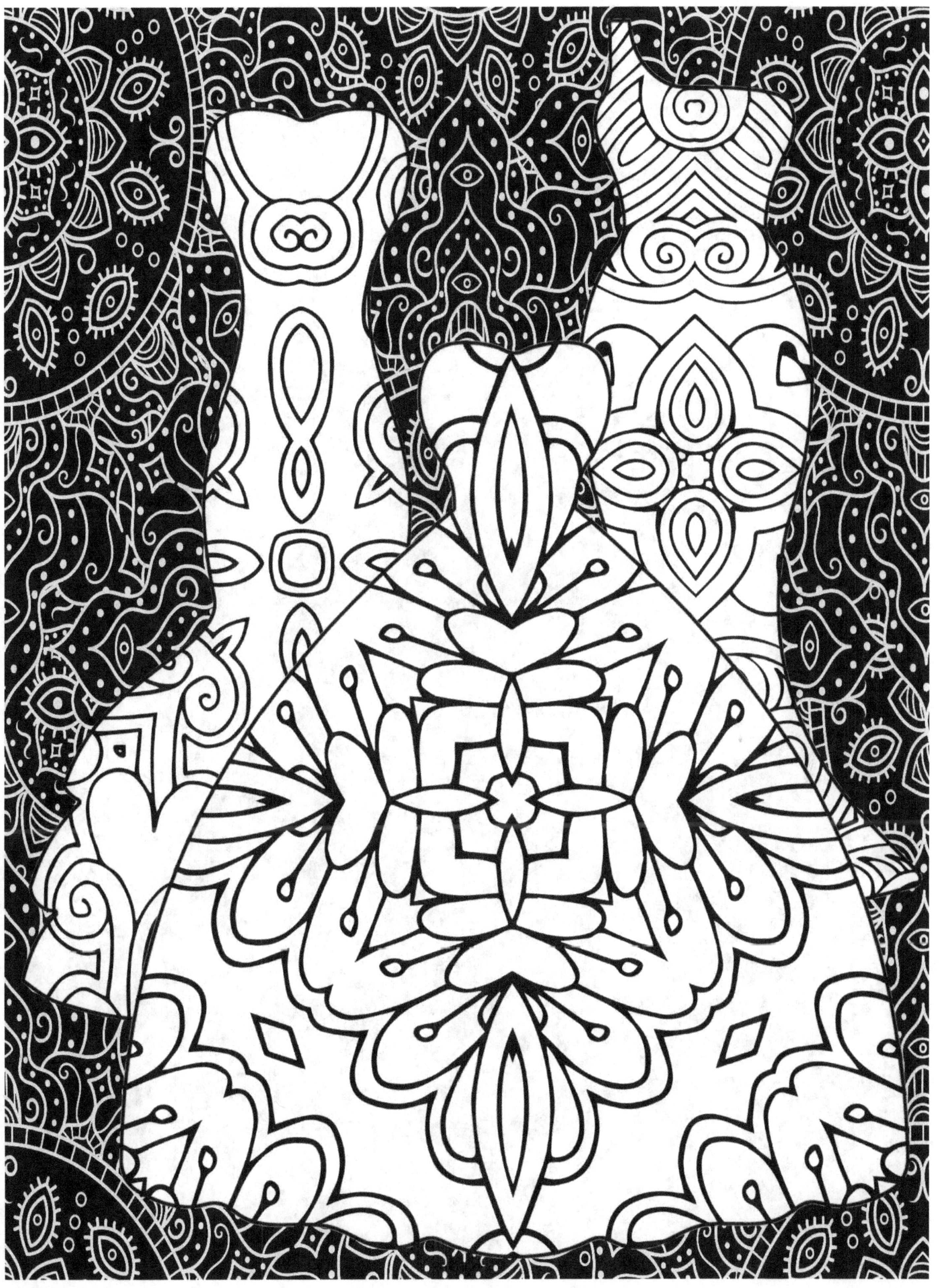

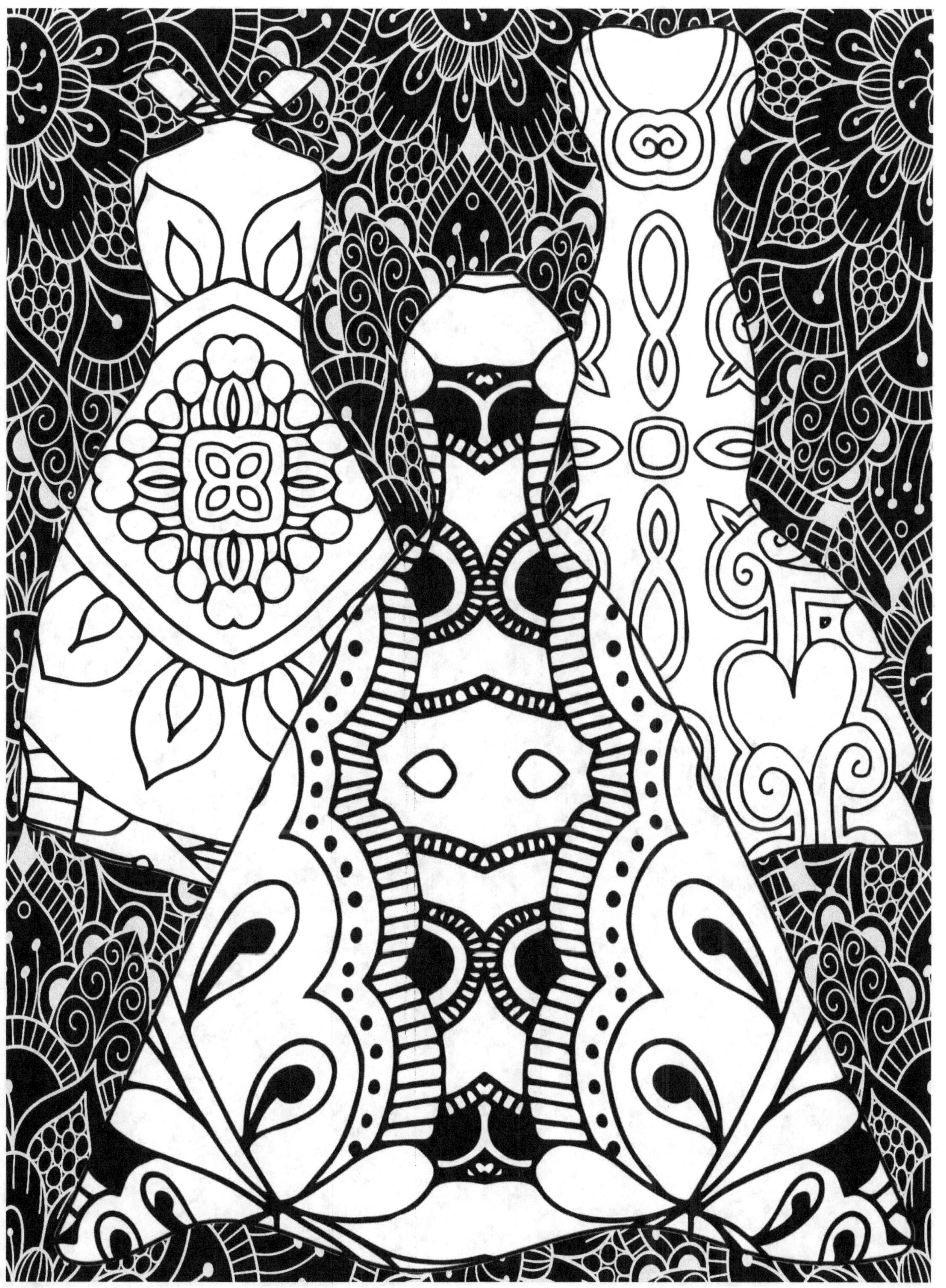

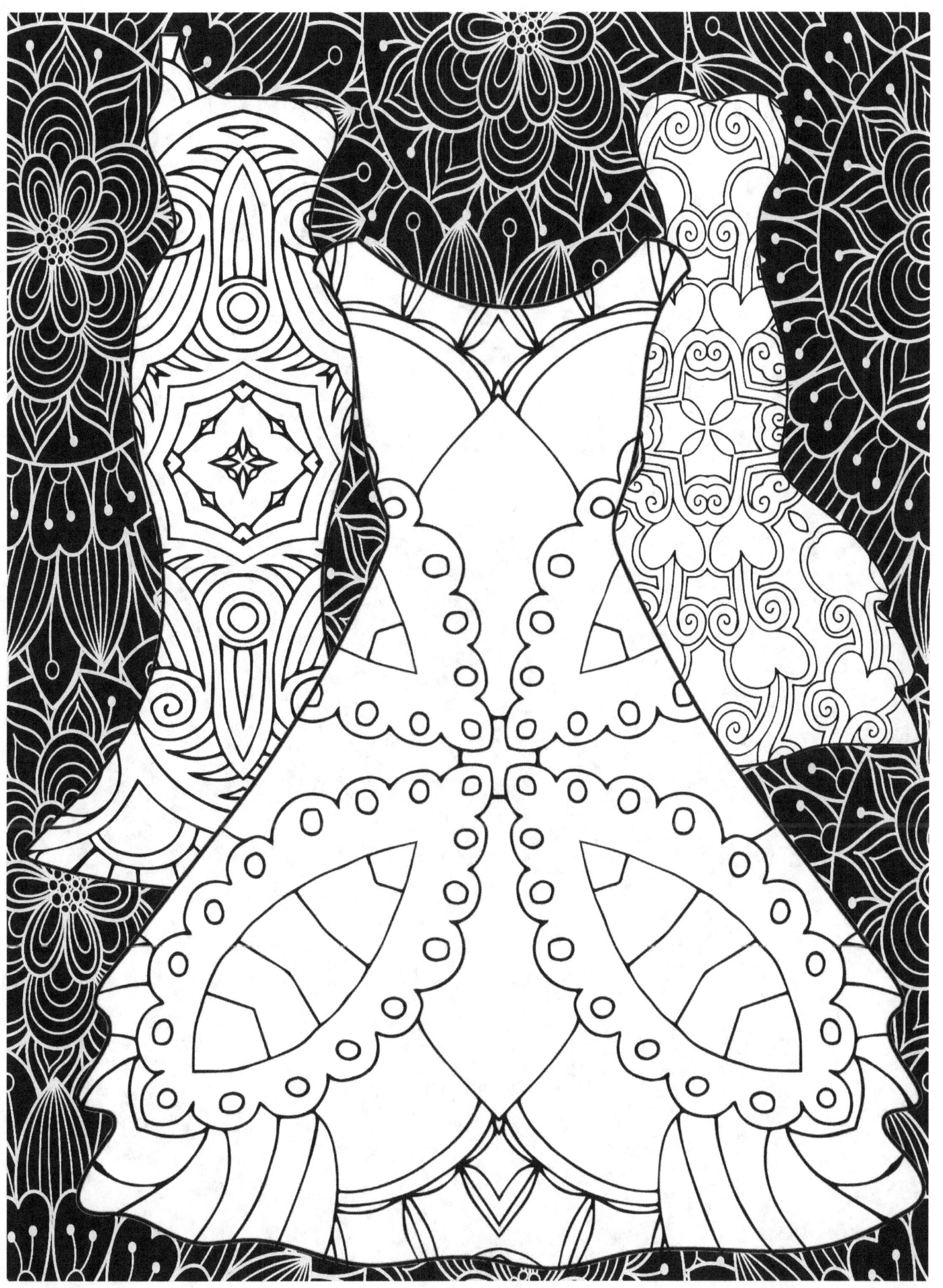

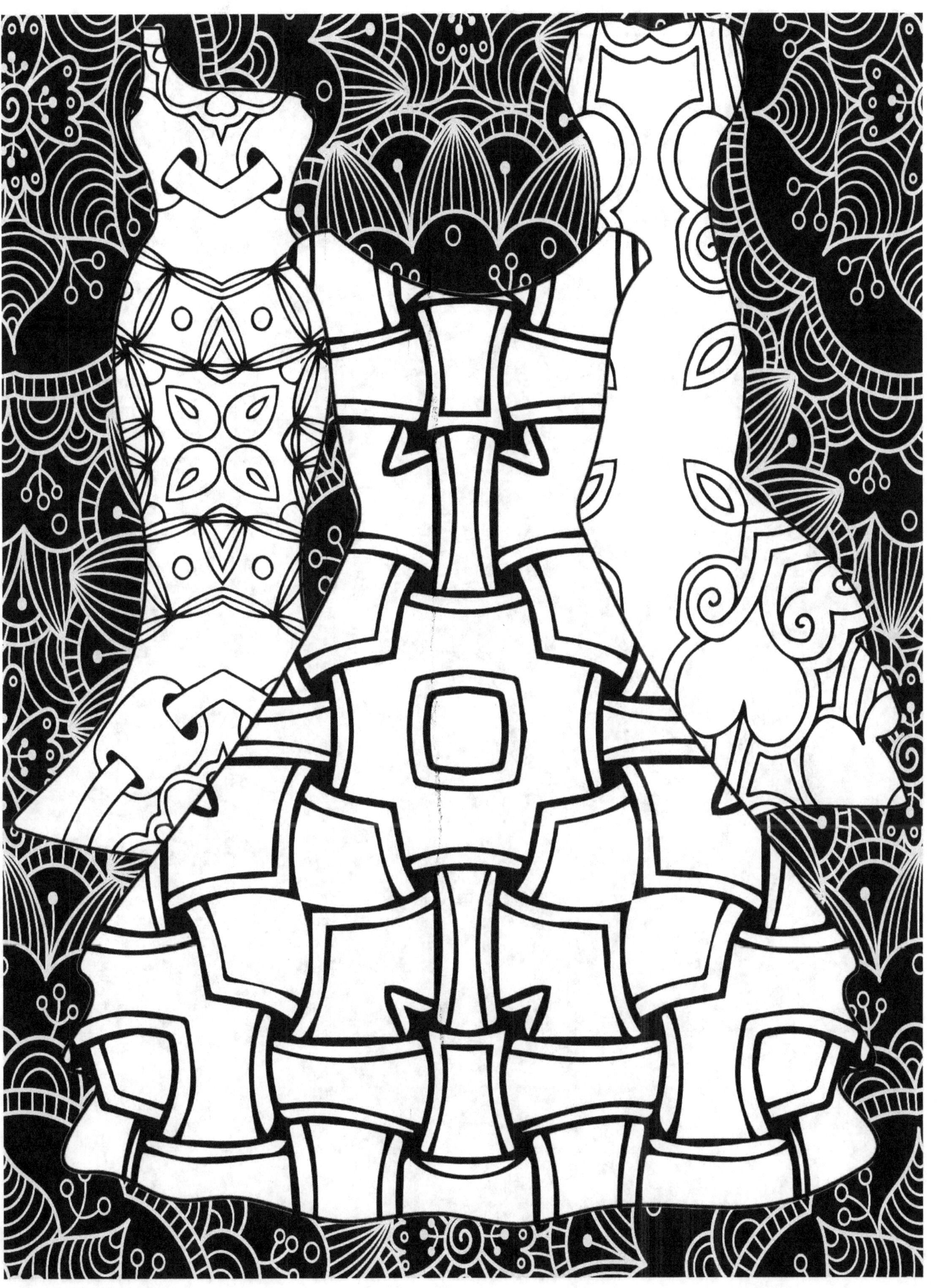

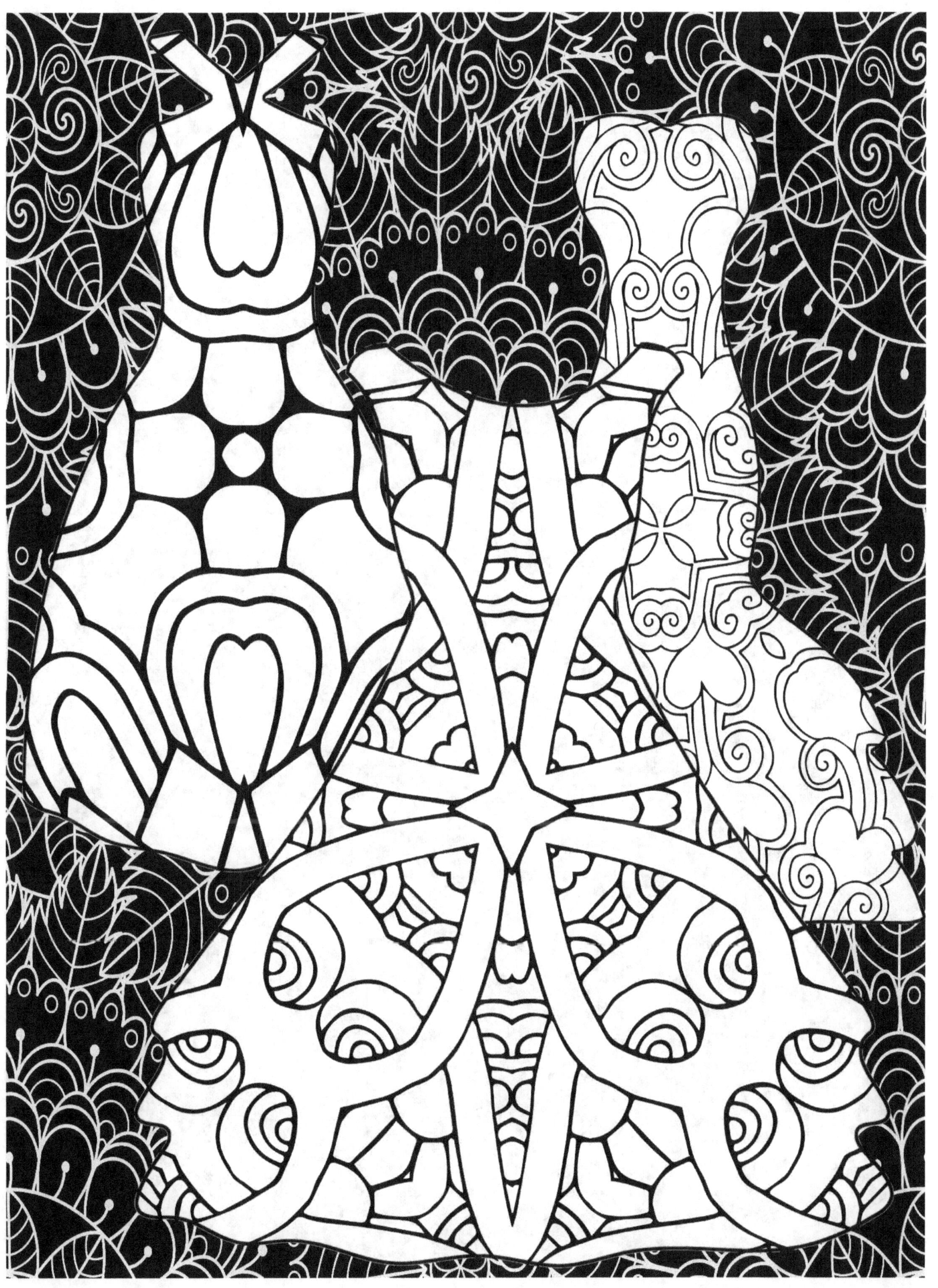

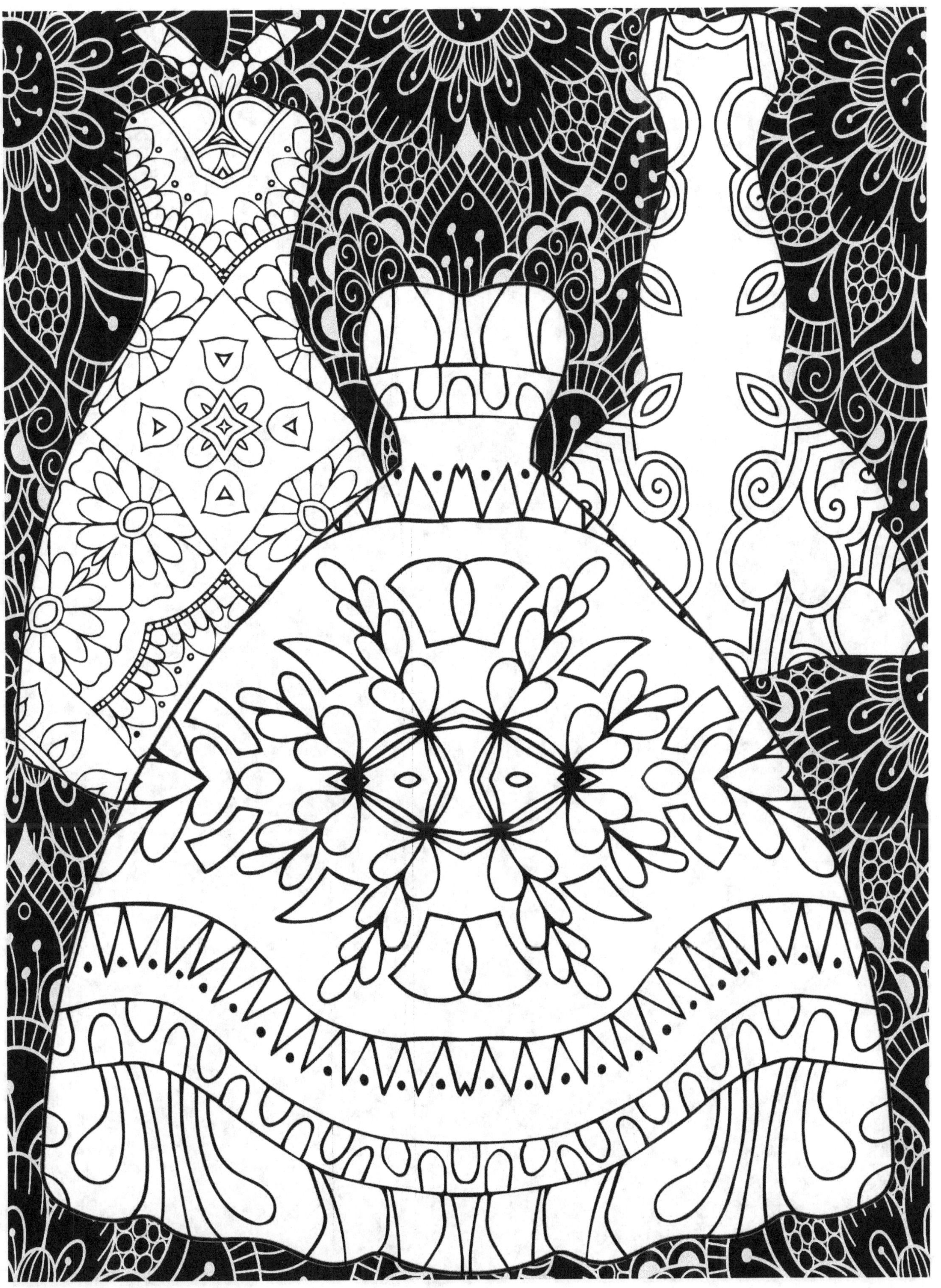

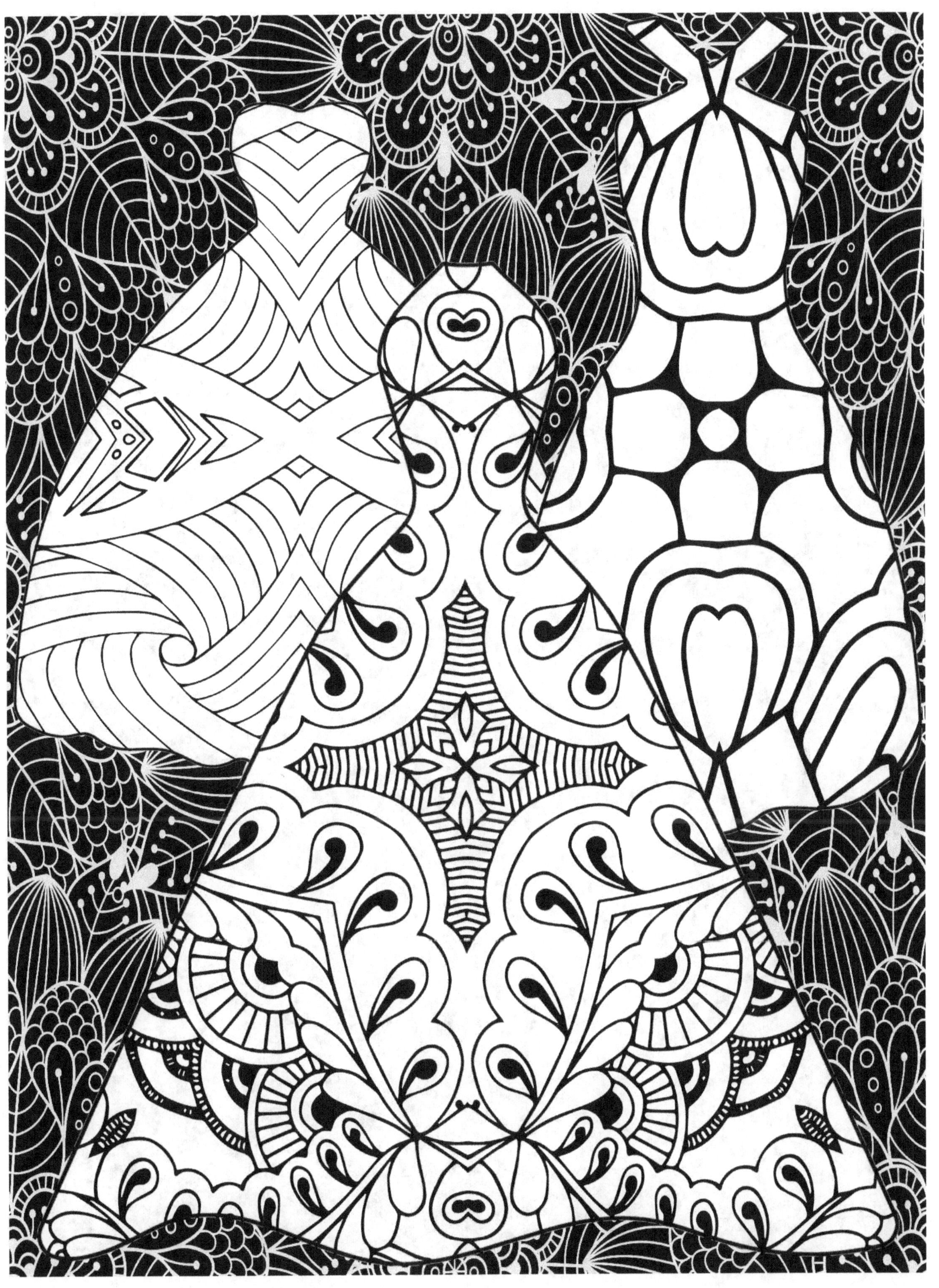

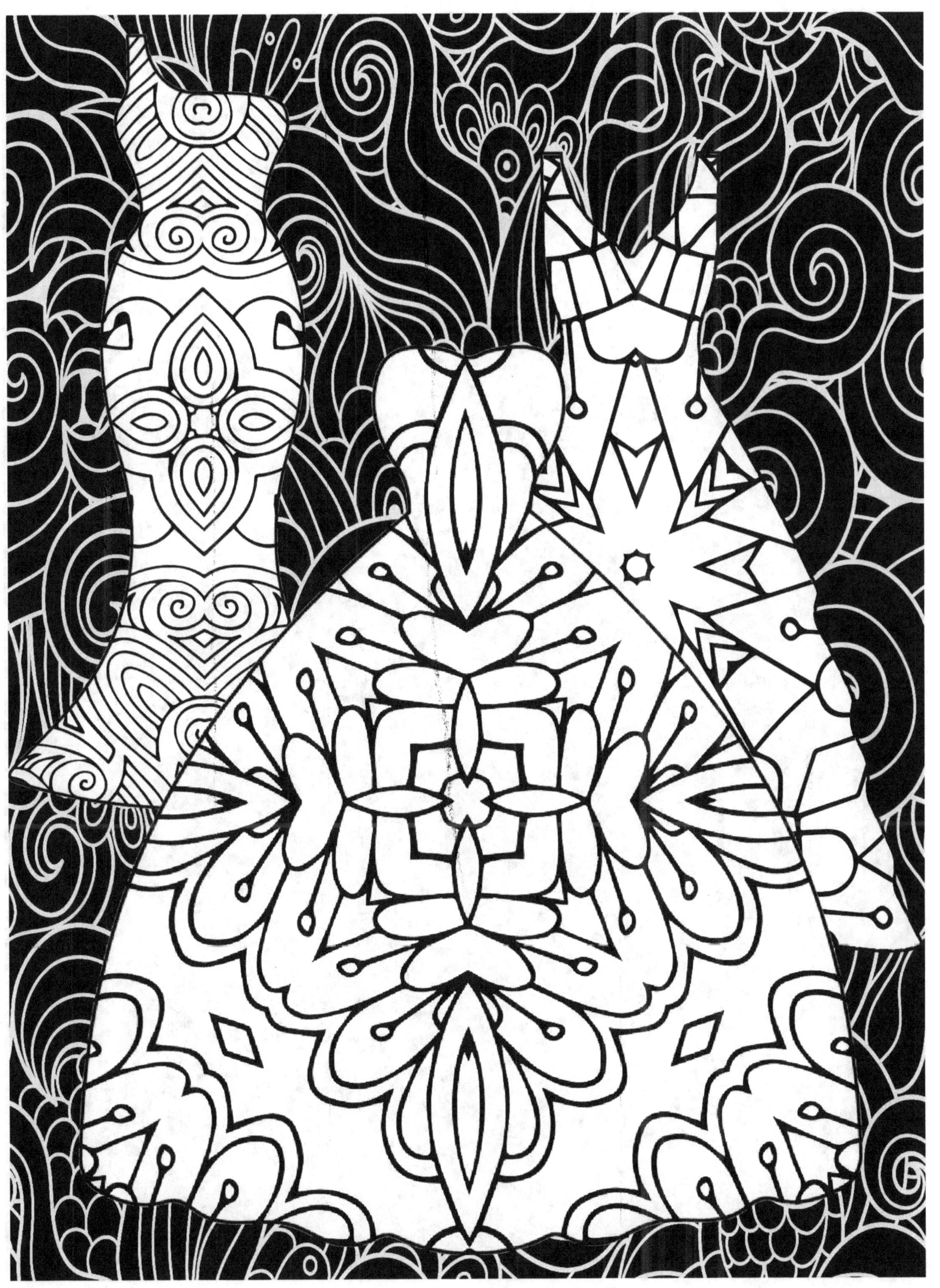

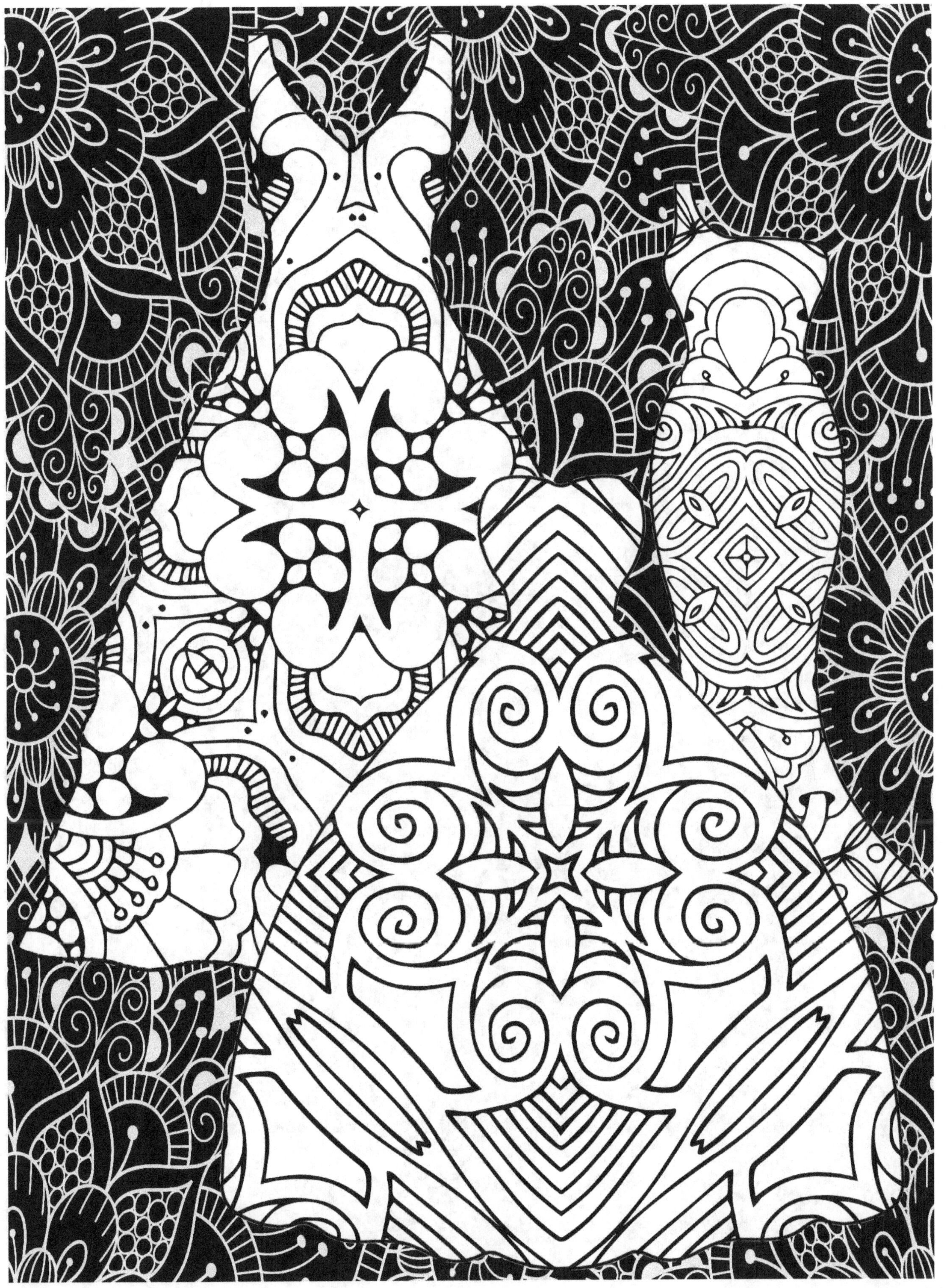

www.ingramcontent.com/pod-product-compliance
Lightning Source LLC
Chambersburg PA
CBHW081729250726
48657CB00010B/3197

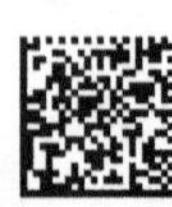
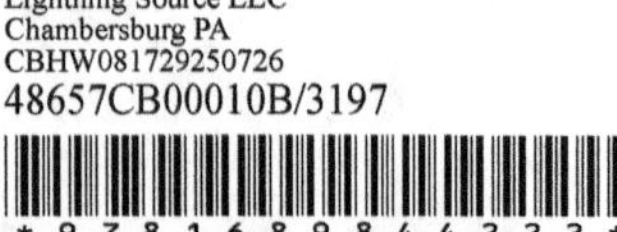